ONLINE BUSINESS GROWTH STRATEGIES

A Practical Nine-Step Guide to Digital Marketing

ONLINE BUSINESS GROWTH STRATEGIES

A Practical Nine-Step Guide to Digital Marketing

FIRST EDITION

David Mitroff, Ph.D.

ABOUT THE AUTHOR

Avid Mitroff, Ph.D. is the Founder and Chief Consultant at Piedmont Avenue Consulting, Inc. (www.PiedmontAve.com), an Oakland, California based award winning business consulting and marketing fir m with a proven track record of producing results.

David and his team advise clients on leveraging technology for creative initiatives from strategy through implementation. David's wealth of knowledge is transferred to clients leading to increased sales, heightened customer experiences and enhanced relationship building techniques.

Dr. Mitroff has an extensive educational background, which includes a Doctorate in Clinical Psychology with coursework in Business Administration, Legal Studies, Marketing, Culinary Arts and professional sales training. This provides a foundation for excellent critical and analytical thinking, business strategy, relationship building and networking.

David is a sought after speaker on a wide range of topics from social media to peak performance. Through his consulting, lectures, trainings and keynotes he has educated more than 35,000+ business owners. He has spoken at events all over the world including in Korea, China, and Turkey for organizations and companies including Google, AT&T and at prestigious conferences including Restaurant Executive Summit, Western Food Service Conference, HardwareCon and the Association of Defense Counsel.

He is a college instructor in Marketing and Entrepreneurship for the University of California at Berkeley International Diploma Program and a Google Mentor for the Google Developers Launchpad Accelerator. David is also a Guest Lecturer at John F. Kennedy University, Diablo Valley College, City College of San Francisco and other colleges.

He has been featured as a business and media expert for NBC, ABC, Forbes, Entrepreneur, Inc. Magazine, Washington Post, Chicago Tribune, The Meeting Professional, Hospitality Technology, California Lawyer and more.

Born in San Francisco and raised in the surrounding cities provides an in-depth personal knowledge of the entire SF Bay Area and a comprehensive network of contacts. To better serve his clients and the community David founded Professional Connector (www. ProfessionalConnector.com) and serves on numerous advisory boards. He enjoys traveling both Domestically (49/50 states) and Internationally (over 40 countries) to share his experiences and bring the world closer to Silicon Valley.

To Ana, Morea, Susan, Mohsin, Patrick, Eric, Janelle, Hannah, Julie, Michelle, Desiree, Chelsea and all the others who have supported me personally and professionally in my business growth.

CONTENTS

FOREWORD
BY PATRICK SCHWERDTFEGER

DIGITAL MARKETING IS easy when you're already famous. All you have to do is be bold, a bit controversial and, ideally, funny. But what do you do if you're not already famous? How do you build an online following if you're just an ordinary person?

This book is designed for the ordinary person and the ordinary business. David Mitroff knows how to leverage online tools to generate traffic, both online and off. His level of expertise is exemplified by his own career path. David came from corporate America and left a good job to start his own consulting firm. Since then, he's amassed an email list in the tens of thousands, held hundreds of business events and attracted clients from all around the world.

The problem with most social media books and training programs is that they don't acknowledge the scrappy "tips and tricks" that generate real results. Instead, they talk about strategic marketing objectives and refining your corporate message. Yes, those things are important, but the real results come from hacking into the social media mindset and giving people an incentive to share your content.

In the end, your customers have to embrace your brand identity voluntarily. They have to carry your torch by choice. Why do people embrace one brand over another? It turns out that there are specific things you can do to create that impact. Mitroff has filled this entire book with examples. It's clear that he built his own online identity from the ground up, and now he's sharing that approach with the world.

Having said that, the book delivers on structure and strategy as well. Mitroff covers nine key areas of online branding, providing "key learnings" as well as specific instructions for each topic. The book provides checklists and guides readers through a methodical marketing playbook. Between this strategic marketing framework, tactical guidance and scrappy tips and tricks, Mitroff delivers a powerful recipe for online success.

The thing I love most about *Online Business Growth Strategies* is the scoring process Mitroff uses to evaluate a business' online reputation. Throughout the book, he shares his scoring methodology, allowing readers to see relevant questions and performance levels to focus on. Not only can readers use these tools to evaluate their own businesses, but they can use them to evaluate competitors as well.

Marketing and branding can be confusing and frustrating at first. Attribution is extremely difficult. John Wanamaker (1838-1922) once said, "Half the money I spend on advertising is wasted; the trouble is, I don't know which half." Mitroff holds nothing back in this book. He shares his considerable experience, allowing readers to formulate sophisticated marketing strategies while maintaining an entrepreneurial approach.

The best use of this book is as a training manual for your marketing department. Rather than hiring a seasoned but expensive marketing manager, hire a recent college grad and arm him/her with this book. It's an instruction manual for online branding. You'll save plenty of time and money as a result. In fact, by following the guidance provided here, your marketing will likely outperform agency alternatives.

Congratulations to you, David Mitroff, for compiling a comprehensive marketing guide while maintaining that essential scrappy flavor. Today's increasingly decentralized marketplace favors clever, unpredictable and entertaining brands. Meanwhile, success depends on consistent and disciplined execution. This book covers both elements, helping ordinary businesses build respectable brands online.

—Patrick Schwerdtfeger

INTRODUCTION

"If I had asked people what they wanted, they would have said, "a faster horse"!"
— Henry Ford, Founder, Ford Motor Company

THE AVERAGE BUSINESS has an online presence which does not represent their product or services accurately. Even worse, when I ask business owners or company managers if they know their website login, over 50% say they do not know. Do you have control over your online presence? Do you have the login ID and Password for your company website? Do you know what shows up when you Google your name or company name? Do you ever wonder why others are ranking higher than your company in Google searches? Are you curious what your current online presence score is compared to other businesses?

Across all industries, regardless of business size, I have found that developing an online presence is a key component in business growth and increase marketplace awareness. This book validates and provides practical examples from my consulting work to demonstrate the importance of creating an online presence by using Social Media and other online tools to leverage business development and marketing strategies. It depicts 9 Key Areas with proven results. People who have applied this system have grown brand awareness, strengthened customer loyalty and increased revenues.

Throughout this book you will hear me mention how fast technology platforms and tactics are changing. I cannot change the speed, however I am confident that I can make sense of online marketing technology and make it easier to manage and leverage. Technology, especially Social Media, is continually changing, making it nearly impossible to have a perfect online presence. However, my consulting firm, Piedmont Avenue Consulting, Inc. (www. PiedmontAve.com) has scored and tracked hundreds of businesses to measure the strength of their online presence. We calculate an Online Presence Score for businesses to determine the impact of its online efforts and identify which areas are most effective and which could use the most improvement.

To do this, we have identified fundamental areas in which a business or organization can use Social Media and other online marketing tools for clear measurable results. This book covers detailed step-by-step methods to assess and improve your business's online presence and then provides "how to" instructions on ways to take your marketing efforts to the next level. This book is broken up into two parts: First the big picture - strategy of defining, assessing and establishing an online presence, and the second the tactics implementing my 9 Key Areas for increasing online presence.

In presenting *Online Business Growth Strategies* to the public, the desire is to help businesses realize the importance of growing their online presence. Most businesses know that they need to create an online presence, but do not know where or how to begin. This book encourages you to actively participate while reading, gaining relevant knowledge about all that you can do to improve your online presence. It is much more than simply understanding your online presence; it includes organizing and promoting events and ways to protect your reputation. Alas, have no fear. After reading this book, you will have a vast understanding of the strategies, tactics and next steps for each of the 9 key areas. You will know how to create a well-functioning website, respond to customer reviews, promote your business in your specific industry and much more.

This book is full of my best business and marketing secrets that I use to grow my clients' businesses, along with materials from hundreds of workshops that I've given on marketing, strategy and entrepreneurship. How much easier would it be for your business to have a guide of 9 key areas to follow to develop an online presence? Each of the key areas has an overview of the topic, key learning objectives, checklist and next steps to follow. In this book readers will find out their current score, receive practical examples to reach online success and uncover numerous free and paid tips and tricks that will help to create a dominating online presence. The higher your online presence score, the more successful your business will be. This book is designed to make an impact.

I have spoken on the topics in this book hundreds of times during keynote talks, workshops, or panels. Initially when I did these talks, I thought that I would inspire and motivate people through my stories — which I included to illustrate what things work and what things do not work from my consulting practice. Overtime, however, I've learned that pain and fear is what causes people to take action. Some of the topics in this book are about the cause and effects of taking or not taking action. For example, if you do not use social media, or you do not engage in most of the techniques in this book, then you are not going to be in business much longer! It takes work, however, it is worth it. If you follow the steps in this book then you are going to be more attractive, make more money, and have greater success.[1]

You can get more detailed information on how to score your business online presence, what your score means, find additional resources to help you grow your business, and request for Piedmont Avenue Consulting, Inc. to review your business by visiting our website at www.PiedmontAve.com/MarketingBook

David Mitroff, Ph.D
www.LinkedIn.com/in/davidmitroff
Consulting: www.PiedmontAve.com
Events: www.ProfessionalConnector.com
Speaking: www.DavidMitroff.com
Office: 510-761-5895
Email: David@PiedmontAve.com

---

1 Based on reviewing my current client list

PART ONE
STRATEGY: ASSESSING AND ESTABLISHING YOUR ONLINE PRESENCE

CHAPTER 1
DEFINING ONLINE PRESENCE

"If opportunity doesn't knock, build a door."
— Milton Berle, Comedian & Actor

BEFORE YOU CAN define your online presence, you have to be able to define who you are, what your business offers, and who your customers are. Most people have the hardest time defining who they are. Since businesses involve people, the classic example to use is "the artist". There is an artist who paints $10,000 beautiful, canvas paintings. Then the artist decides they would like to begin working digitally and make logos even though they have not made or sold logos before. The artist cannot sell logos for $10,000, especially if they are new at digital design; they could probably charge around $500. The artist is now selling a $10,000 painting, but a $500 logo. If people go to Google to try and find the artist, how does the artist distinguish themselves in this scenario? In my experience, it takes time to identify who you are, what you do, and how you work. In one scenario, you might create two websites, one for traditional art and another for branding and graphic design. The alternative would be one site for all the artists' different types of work, which says that you are an artist that specializes in canvas paintings, who also does digital branding and logos. It does take time, however once you claim ownership of your brand, things will come together.

In my case, I have a PhD in Clinical Psychology, however, I studied and worked in a variety of other areas such as sales and marketing. A lot of times people are confused about how I switched from psychology to marketing. My answer is that psychology is marketing. I claimed ownership over that belief. Overtime, as I have grown and developed my business model, people no longer question the validity of that bridge between psychology and marketing because I have mastered both simultaneously, together, as my brand and business. The same thing goes for the artist. It just so happens that people can be passionate about painting, making logos and branding all at the same time. This leads you to be able to distinguish yourself, your brand and your company.

What is Online Presence?

An online presence used to be a website, a small, unconnected mirror. The existence of your business or brand online goes far beyond your website. These days, like it or not, everyone has an online presence. How good you are at developing an online presence comes down to the magnitude of how well you draw traffic to your business through different online resources. Anything that can be done through an online search to find your business, this can be labeled as online presence. Due to the numerous factors that come into play when creating an online presence, there are different ways that a company can leverage and enhance their existing online presence to further boost exposure, develop a reputation and market themselves online.

What is Social Media?

Social Media is the biggest component of creating an online presence. It now intrudes on every aspect of our personal and professional life. Social media is a collection of online communication channels that allow for interaction, unique and personalized creations, content sharing and partnership with people and businesses worldwide. Social media is a combination of websites and applications that empower users to create and share content or to partake in social networking.

Social media makes information more accessible and useful by combining together technology, content and social interaction in many forms. This includes the use of websites, blogs, podcasts, video and photo sharing, social bookmarking, microblogs, review sites, instant messaging, mobile apps, business networks, forums and many other social networks.

Social media, more than ever, is such a large part of everyone's lives, so much that both individuals and companies must set clear guidelines and objectives to avoid any unintentional issues that might effect their reputation. If used skillfully, social media is one of the most powerful tools we can leverage to create new opportunities. Because social media is about feedback, listening, and sharing, you will learn how to attract more business, and in doing so reach a broader audience, receive more referrals, and maintain customer loyalty. Social Media is a two-way street that gets better the more you engage with it.

What is Search Engine Optimization?

Search Engine Optimization, or SEO for short, is the strategies and tactics used to increase visitor traffic to a website by getting higher rankings in search result pages on Google, Yahoo, etc. Search results are in the millions, and most visitors don't look past the first page of Search Results. The closer your website link and other online materials is to the top of the Search Results list, the more likely visitors will click and consequently be exposed to your brand.

What is Conversation Rate Optimization?

Conversation Rate Optimization, or CRO for short, is a methodology of creating an experience for a webpage visitor that influences them to become a customer. CRO promotes a response from the visitor. SEO helps you get discovered (via search) and CRO measures actions customers take once they are on your webpage.

What Are the Benefits of Increasing Your Online Presence?

From the biggest multi-nationals to the smallest mom-and-pops corner stores, an online presence today is considered fundamental. Online, meaning most of your customers and potential customers walking by right now are on their phones looking at your online presence.

Social validation increases purchasing likelihood. The Internet gives consumers a platform to connect with others and be exposed to their likes, dislikes, interests and much more. This real-time and immediate communication gives companies the opportunity to use each platform to market and advertise its products or services to its target market. The benefits of an online presence include:

- Increased exposure
- Increased traffic
- Development of brand loyalty
- Provide marketplace insight and research
- Generate leads
- Create business partnerships and collaborations
- Establish thought leadership
- Improved sales process

How Can Having a Bigger Online Presence Increase Revenue?

The use of the web can increase sales in today's marketplace because of its immense reach and clear trajectory into the mainstream of our digital lives. The following statistics[2] show the importance and value of the Internet:

- On a daily basis, Facebook users share 4.75 billion pieces of content (web links, news stories, blog posts, notes, photos, etc.)

---

2 *See the Reference section at the end of the book for further information and sources*

- 63.4% of social sellers reported an increase in their company's sales revenue vs. only 41.2% of non-social sellers

- 92% of consumer's trust earned media such as peer recommendations and word-of-mouth and 70% of global consumers indicate that they trust online consumer reviews

- 74% of consumers rely on social media to inform their purchasing decisions

- 77% of B2B technology decision-makers are active on social media

- As of June 2016, Twitter has 1 billion unique visits monthly to sites with embedded tweets

- Nearly 80% of all social media time is spent on mobile apps or websites

- Social media advertising revenue will reached $9.8 billion by the end of 2016

- 33% of millennials identify social media as one of their preferred channels for communicating with business

- 64% of sales professionals closed at least 1 deal in 2014 as a direct result of using social media

Key Learning - Online presence impacts purchasing behaviors, strengthens customer loyalty, enables reputation management, opens new sales channels and creates a larger following than one could achieve by only interacting with people directly. The people online having conversations about you and your business become hundreds of individual spokespersons and salespeople for your brand and company.

Checklist:

- ❑ What are your current social media efforts?

- ❑ What parts of your business can be effected by your online presence?

- ❑ Do you have an Online Brand/Branding Strategy?

- ❑ What components of your marketing plan could you add social media to?

- ❑ Social Media and online presence is a hopeful frontier, but a monster to tackle. I'm going to teach you how! Are you ready?

Next Step: We will next introduce how to measure the value of increasing your online presence and social media for your business, along with strategies for increasing revenues.

CHAPTER 2
MEASURING THE VALUE OF AN ONLINE PRESENCE

"The Internet is becoming the town square for the global village of tomorrow. Creativity is allowing yourself to make mistakes. Art is knowing which ones to keep."

— Scott Adams, Creator of the syndicated Dilbert Cartoon

OVER THE YEARS of mentoring people and consulting with companies, I have seen the increased importance of growing an online presence. Nowadays everyone goes online to check you and your business out, whether they are going to give you funding, go eat at your restaurant, hire you, anything. Consumers have the ability to access information about your business in an instance. What you want to do is figure out how valuable your online presence is and how you can improve the value of your online presence. Before you can go forward, you need to understand where you are at with your online presence by measuring it in order to capitalize on certain key variables that will lead your business to more opportunities. Without measurement, there can be no progress.

How Do We Measure the Value of Online Presence?

An effective online presence can build brand awareness and help to increase sales and services. Many social media platforms began as an entertainment and progressed into a powerful marketing weapons. Each individual business will have different online objectives that will vary based upon the industry it operates in. Nonetheless, the value of the web does not change.

Online Objectives May Include:

- Customer loyalty programs
- Testimonials from satisfied customers
- Establishing trust and authenticity
- Increased referrals
- "Word of Mouth" and "Front of Mind" advertising
- Immediate feedback about products or services
- Business promotion to a larger audience
- Market research

Value of Conversations

Social media platforms are often used for personal online conversations. However, when used for business conversations, the results can be measured the same way as other business development and marketing efforts. By strategically placing content and encouraging conversations online about your brand, the online community tells your story, explains your value proposition and creates awareness. This leads to sales both in the short term and in the long term.

In this case, your online customers are selling your products and services to their peers, without you paying them. Quit thinking of the Internet as purely public relations, customer service, or a customer relationship management tool.

Key Learning - With a clear strategic plan, your online presence can result in creating awareness and increasing sales in the same way that sales representatives, marketing managers, focus group facilitators, in store managers and others are paid to have conversations about your business.

Checklist:

❑ How valuable is feedback from your customers for your success?

❑ Are you continually reaching new market segments (such as the mobile marketplace)?

❑ How strong is your marketplace presence?

Next Step: We next examine the Online Marketing Budget by looking at the current trends and the best areas to invest in your business future.

CHAPTER 3
ONLINE MARKETING BUDGET

"There is no such thing as a free lunch."
— *Milton Friedman, Economist*

- Will Online Marketing result in more customers visiting a business and requesting products and services? **YES.**
- Can Online Marketing improve the overall positive views of the business? **YES.**
- Does Online Marketing lead to greater sales? **YES.**
- Can we measure the Online Marketing Return on Investment (ROI)? **YES.**
- Do we need a budget for Online Marketing? **YES.**

JUST LIKE IT is important to set a budget for every other aspect of your business operations, it is no different for online spending. The Internet is so prominent in today's society that it is important to set a budget accordingly. Organizations are rapidly shifting their marketing budget to allocate an increase to their social media efforts to meet the escalating importance it plays in their overall marketing mix.

EXAMPLES

Social Media Spending[3]

- Organizations worldwide spent approximately $16 billion U.S. in 2014 on social media advertising. Investments in this area are meant to almost double by 2016, reaching $31 billion U.S.

- Share of marketing budget spent on social media is expected to double by 2020 from 11% today to 24%

- The U.S. is the largest social media advertising market in the world by far

- 57.5% of small businesses spend $26 or more per month on tools to publish and analyze their social media

"How Much Do I Spend?"

When it comes to your online marketing budget, there is both time and money to be considered. How much time are you willing to spend posting to Twitter, Facebook, Newsletters, connecting on LinkedIn, adding new content to your website, etc. How much time and energy are you willing to spend, when is it worth it, when is it not, and how do you decide? Cost = the time, money, attention, and consistency, reorienting our hard-boiled conceptions.

Every industry has its own audience to serve. Depending on your business needs, social media expenses can include design and graphics, audience research, advertising, scheduling, analytics and more. It is important to set online objectives and tailor the budget around these activities. Keep in mind that you want to spend money on activities that take the most time to do and/or the activities that your organization does not do well. That way you are maximizing your efficiency. Every action for the budget must be organized around activities that will lead to your business making more money.

---

3 *See the Reference section at the end of the book for further information and sources*

Validating Social Media

To validate using social media as a key component in the development strategy and marketing plan, it is critical that businesses evaluate the amount of money spent on social media and the sales developed from it. 53% of social media marketers don't measure their success[4]. It is critical when establishing any marketing goals or efforts to have clear marketing metrics that can be easily tracked and measured. For example you may want to track how many new customer leads you get each day, each week, each month and each quarter. Then track what sources these leads came from (Yelp, website, referrals, etc.). Based on this data you can track what marketing outreach is most effective, seasonal changes in your business from year to year and much more.

Key Learning - Although it might be difficult to directly correlate a sale to a post on a social media network, social media managers must frequently monitor things such as traffic, number of fans and followers, reviews, mentions and shares, etc. to make sure its efforts are successful.

Social media is not a fad. It is a reality. Organizations can cultivate success by developing its budget and strategies surrounding this form of marketing. Increasing your business investments in social media is beneficial because it is:

- Low cost marketing

- Essential for success

- Directly engaging customers

- A platform to publicize your business ethics

Social media has become a necessity for marketing campaigns.

---

4 *See the Reference section at the end of the book for further information and sources*

CHAPTER 4
ASSESSMENT OF CURRENT BUSINESS MARKETING STRATEGY

"Only the best is good enough."
— *Ole Kirk Christiansen, Founder, LEGO Group*

THIS QUESTIONNAIRE BELOW includes general questions about your goals, current and past marketing efforts, branding strategy, evaluating completion, budget, time and more relevant inquiries. The goal is for these questions to make you think what is currently working, as well some areas that could be improved. Regardless of the type of business, you need to first assess who your customers are and ask the right questions to avoid critical mistakes. Dana Mitroff (2017) goes into great depth about critical mistakes made by beginning design thinkers in *Five mistakes of Beginning Design Thinker (And How To Overcome Them)*. She refers to design thinking as being "grounded in understanding people," meaning your consumers, customer, and market. Without understanding the needs of those you are trying to reach, your business goals will most likely never be reached. I have used this set of questions to help 100's of clients and businesses understand and honestly evaluate their online marketing needs and requirements.

The way we work at Piedmont Avenue Consulting, Inc. is typically offering a free phone call consultation. If you go to our website, you can schedule a free consultation call, or if you meet me in person then I would tell you that the first step is this phone call. So routinely we have these phone calls with people or companies, offering them ideas and suggestions on how they can improve and grow their business, or optimize their organization, etc. Based on that, the next step is a more comprehensive assessment. Prior to the assessment, we require businesses to fill out this questionnaire. The assessment in about a two-hour meeting (could be in person, on phone call, or over Skype) where we analyze the work you have done on your business and brand thus far, and how we can help you improve. This session would be charged for, but it allows businesses to really start to see the immediate opportunity for growth within their company. There would be ideas that are free; such as if you have one category on Yelp—add two more, or adding missing components onto your website. Then there are other things that cost money, like a sandwich board, or A-frame outside of your business, setting up an email newsletters, etc. It is not about paying us, there are things that you have to do that cost money. During the assessment, we come up with those ideas then help people implement those strategies.

What I have included in Chapter 4 is some of the questions that we ask during the assessment, because I think it is important for you as a business to assess where you are at and based on that we can move into implementation.

Please review and complete this questionnaire to help you assess your current situation. You can also find a word document of our comprehensive questionnaire to download at www.PiedmontAve. com/MarketingBook

Current Marketing Efforts (traditional and new media marketing)

- What are your past and present marketing activities?

- Which ones worked? Which ones didn't?

- Do you have funds set aside for marketing? If yes, how much money do you realistically have for marketing your product/ service? If no, are you interested in a loan?

- Do you currently have a customer loyalty program (email marketing, monthly newsletter, size of email list, etc.)?

- Do you have an event calendar on your website, in emails or promote events to the community?

- Who controls your website(s)? What website pages do you have content on or can you have changed? Do you have the ability to change the look of the site?

- How often do you update your social media networks (Facebook, Twitter, LinkedIn, etc.)?

- Are you in partnership with any associations, groups, conferences or chambers?

Branding and Customer Experience

- What first impression are you trying to create with your brand? (e.g. established, safe, cutting edge, friendly, easy to use, trendy, etc.)

- What's the problem your product or service helps solve for your customers or what opportunity does it allow them to take advantage of?

- What products and/or services do you provide? Please provide a brief explanation.

- Who are your customers/clients for each of the products and services above (e.g. size of targeted companies or customer demographics such as primarily male or female, age range or income level, etc.)?

Competition

Who are your competitors or perceived competitors? List at least 3 with their websites... and don't say you don't have any. List anything in particular you may like, may not like or stands out to you that is important for us to know about your competition.

- Which one are you most concerned about?

- Is your business in a relatively competitive/saturated market or are there only a handful of companies making the same/similar offer?

- Are you priced the same, lower or higher than competitors?

Key Learning - When working on your marketing strategy you want to make sure that your strategy includes actions you or your team enjoy working on. You want to have fun!! I always say "if it's not fun you're not going to do it".

CHAPTER 5
9 KEYS TO INCREASING YOUR ONLINE PRESENCE

"We don't have a choice on whether we DO social media, the question is how well we DO it."

— *Erik Qualman, Author*

I N 2010, I began my journey to help companies develop their online presence by going door to door on Union Street in the San Francisco, CA Marina District. From traditional companies (retail, restaurants, hotels, etc.) to professional organizations (law firms, startups, entrepreneurs, etc.), I tried explaining to these business owners that by increasing their online presence they could help their organizations grow. I was kicked out of every company I stepped inside, hearing things like "Social Media is just noise" and "Growing an online presence isn't a priority for businesses." Determined to share my expertise, I developed the 9 Keys as an easy tool for organizations to follow, as well as an online presence scoresheet that rates and scores how effective and efficient a company is at utilizing the power of Social Media. I then scored the entire Union Street using the 9 Keys and presented the scores to owners. When owners saw their data-driven score compared to other nearby businesses, they began to understand the power of digital branding, and this finally gained traction in the minds of business owners.

As we have covered, social media is an essential component of developing an online presence and reaching success in any industry. At Piedmont Avenue Consulting, Inc. (www.PiedmontAve.com), we have found that social media is vital for all of our clients. Having a perfect social media presence is nearly impossible because of the nature of its industry (new technologies and platforms regularly being developed). We measure social media presence to determine the influence of an organization's online efforts. We identify which areas are most effective and which could use the most improvement.

How Do You Measure Social Media Presence?

Piedmont Avenue Consulting, Inc. has scored and tracked hundreds of businesses to measure the strength of their social media presence. To do this, we have identified 9 Key areas a business or organization can use social media for measurable results. You will notice that some platforms fit under more than one key area based upon its characteristics.

Key Area of an Online Presence	Examples (will vary by industry)
1. Website & Blog	WordPress, Wix, Weebly, Blogger
2. Online Directory	Google My Business, Google Maps, Yahoo! Local, Yellow Pages, Bing, Yelp, CitySearch, Angie's List
3. Review Sites	Yelp, Angie's List, Google Reviews/ Zagat, Amazon, TripAdvisor
4. Social Networks	Facebook, LinkedIn, Google+
5. Microblogging	Twitter, Tumblr
6. Rich Media	YouTube, iTunes, SoundCloud, Podcasts, Spotify, Flickr, Snapchat, Instagram, Vine, Vimeo, Pinterest
7. Mobile Marketing	Mobile Apps, SMS Text, Foursquare
8. Industry Specific	Lawyers.com, Expedia, Vitals.com, Healthgrades.com, Diablo Magazine, Oakland Magazine, San Francisco Chronicle, SF Business Times
9. Event Marketing, offline/online	Meetup, Eventbrite, Constant Contact, FullCalendar

For each key area identified, we have developed detailed, industry-specific criteria on which we base our scores and track our clients. These criteria include questions such as:

- How often is the business's Facebook page updated?

- Are there photos on the Google My Business page?

- Has the business been featured in any local or national media?

- Are consumers given an avenue to provide reviews?

Online Presence Scoresheet

On a 900-point scale (100 possible for each of the 9 key areas) the average total score for the businesses we have scored is only 285, indicating the online marketplace is underutilized and there is a huge amount of room for improvement.

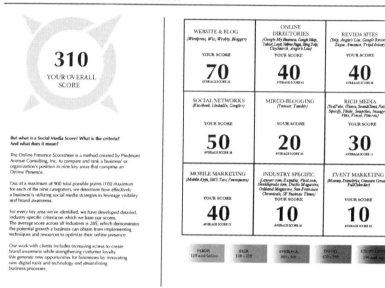

YOUR ONLINE PRESENCE SCORESHEET

310
YOUR OVERALL SCORE

But what is a Social Media Score? What is the criteria? And what does it mean?

The Online Presence Scoresheet is a method created by Piedmont Avenue Consulting, Inc. to compare and rank a business' or organization's position in nine key areas that comprise an Online Presence.

Out of a maximum of 900 total possible points (100 maximum for each of the nine categories), we determine how effectively a business is utilizing social media strategies to leverage visibility and brand awareness.

For every key area we've identified, we have developed detailed, industry-specific criteria on which we base our scores. The average score across all industries is 285, which demonstrates the potential growth a business can obtain from implementing techniques and resources to optimize their online presence.

Our work with clients includes increasing scores to create brand awareness while strengthening customer loyalty. We generate new opportunities for businesses by innovating new digital tools and technology and streamlining business processes.

WEBSITE & BLOG	ONLINE DIRECTORIES	REVIEW SITES
YOUR SCORE **70**	YOUR SCORE **40**	YOUR SCORE **40**
SOCIAL NETWORKS	MICRO-BLOGGING	RICH MEDIA
YOUR SCORE **50**	YOUR SCORE **20**	YOUR SCORE **30**
MOBILE MARKETING	INDUSTRY SPECIFIC	EVENT MARKETING
YOUR SCORE **40**	YOUR SCORE **10**	YOUR SCORE **10**

Next Step: To help you navigate the online ecosystem we provide more details, along with strategic concepts and action items for each of the nine key areas.

Now you have two ways to utilize the book at this point. One option is to score your business right now. The other option is to score your business as you are reading the chapter relating to that specific key.

You can also get more detailed information on what your score means, find additional resources to help you grow your business and request for Piedmont Avenue Consulting, Inc. to review your business by visiting our website at www.PiedmontAve.com/MarketingBook

CHAPTER 6
WHAT'S YOUR SCORE?

THERE ARE TWO ways to utilize the book at this point. Right here and now you can score your business across the 9 Keys to see where your business is at with its online presence. The other option, or you can do both, is to score your business as you're reading each chapter pertaining to that specific key. If you score your business now, you will have a baseline that you can use as you go through.

Looking at these nine keys, how does your business' Online Presence rank?

1. Your Website & Blog Score = _____ on page 45
2. Your Online Directory Score = _____ on page 56
3. Your Review Sites Score = _____ on page 64
4. Your Social Networks Score = _____ on page 74
5. Your Microblogging Score = _____ on page 85
6. Your Rich Media Score = _____ on page 97
7. Your Mobile Marketing Score = _____ on page 113
8. Your Industry Specific Score = _____ on page 120
9. Your Event Marketing Score = _____ on page 138

Add these 9 key area scores to calculate:

TOTAL = _____

Now that you know your score, it's time to understand it. As you will notice, 90 was the highest score you could reach on each of the 9 Key Areas. This is because it is impossible to get a perfect score. With technology constantly changing, businesses can always be doing *more*.

YOUR ONLINE PRESENCE SCORESHEET

WEBSITE & BLOG	ONLINE DIRECTORIES	REVIEW SITES
YOUR SCORE	YOUR SCORE	YOUR SCORE
SOCIAL NETWORKS	MIRCO-BLOGGING	RICH MEDIA
YOUR SCORE	YOUR SCORE	YOUR SCORE
MOBILE MARKETING	INDUSTRY SPECIFIC	EVENT MARKETING
YOUR SCORE	YOUR SCORE	YOUR SCORE

YOUR OVERALL SCORE

EXCELLENT:	550 and up
GOOD:	450 - 549
AVERAGE:	260 - 449
FAIR:	120 - 259
POOR:	119 and below

If you have a score of:

- 119 or below = POOR

  o Requires significant improvement

- 120-259 = FAIR

  o Needs to be developed further

- 260-449 = AVERAGE

  o In line with what most other companies are doing. As you can see, there is still immense room for improvement

- 430-549 = GOOD

  o You are above the curve

- 550 and up = EXCELLENT

  o You are among the very few who reach this level. Props to your business for taking advantage of Social Media and for developing your online presence

As I mentioned earlier, on a 900-point scale (100 possible for each of the 9 key areas) the average total score for the businesses we have scored is only 285. This indicates a substantial amount of room for improvement and showcases how underutilized the online market-place is. You can get more detailed information on what your score means, find additional resources to help you grow your business and request for Piedmont Avenue Consulting, Inc. to review your business by visiting our website at www.PiedmontAve.com/MarketingBook

What's Your Score?

Rate your business based upon the answers to the previous questions.

How Many You Have		Score
0	=	0
1-3	=	30
4-6	=	60
7-9	=	80
10+	=	90

Your Review Sites Score = _____

PART TWO
TACTICS: IMPLEMENTING YOUR MARKETING VISION
WITH DAVID MITROFF'S 9 KEYS TO INCREASE YOUR
ONLINE PRESENCE

CHAPTER 7
KEY 1
WEBSITE & BLOG

"Building a mission and building a business go hand in hand."

— Mark Zuckerberg, Founder, Facebook

TODAY, MOST ORGANIZATIONS have a website and its is often the first impression your business makes on a potential customer. In regards to a business's online presence, the website is the most important of the 9 key areas because it defines your company, your message to customers and establishes credibility for your business. The company website also acts as a central hub, providing links to all your other sites. The best part of having a website is that you are in control of it. A blog is a webpage that has regularly updated content. It enables you to communicate the identity of your company, giving yourself a chance to tell your own story.

Examples of Website and Blog Platforms

WordPress, Wix, Weebly, Blogger, Medium

Benefits of a Website and Blog

There are many reasons why companies need a website and a blog. The following express why a website and blog are beneficial to a company:

- Create your own content - It is dedicated space where you are able to control the content and story being told about your business

- It is an outlet for you to define a clear message and express what you offer - It is important to maintain consistency in theme and information

- These sites allow you to create a medium for contact – invite feedback, comments, consumer interaction, provide customer experience surveys and email newsletter sign ups

- A place to provide links to related pages - Make it simple for customers to follow you across multiple social media platform such as Twitter, Facebook, etc.

Key Learning - Focus on including the message you want to send out, the direct connection to engage connectivity, keeping information both interesting and current, the look and feel of your site, the ease and accessibility of your site and the "call to action" that encourages business.

Developing a Website

Creating an effective website is not a simple task, but can be made easy with the right tactics in mind. We have put together 6 objectives a business can do to enhance their website, making it aesthetically pleasing to its audience and draw in traffic:

1. **Have a Clear Message:** A clear message will help you define what you want to offer to those visiting your site. How your website

looks aesthetically also reflects what type of message you are sending. The home page or landing page of your website needs to showcase your brand and purpose, clearly define what products and services you offer and provide an interesting background that sets the company apart from the rest. These factors are the most important information people look for when visiting any site. If they are not present on your homepage visitors may not take the time to explore the rest of your site in order to find the information they are looking for. This results in a lost prospect.

2. **Two-Way Communication/Contact Us:** Once a clear message has been established for the home page, the next step is to create a medium for contact. It is important to make it easy for visitors to leave feedback, ask questions and converse with other visitors on your website. An easy way to create a connection with website visitors is to create a prompt to collect the visitor's contact information, such as email, to later connect with them regarding events, promotions and/or newsletters.

    A company website can best produce results by including contact forms throughout the entire website to make it as easy as possible for visitors to reach you. The basics for contact information forms include email, phone number and physical address. Additional contact information can include a section for visitors to leave feedback, give comments, or ask questions.

3. **Provide Links to Your Other Pages:** Showing your visitors that you are connected all over the web by linking your Facebook, Twitter, Instagram, etc. on your website will increase credibility of your brand. Create a clear icon or button for each link to your other sites on the homepage, where they will be easily accessible and quick to find.

4. **Update the Content and Maintain a Consistent Look:** Make sure the theme of your website is consistent across all pages to create a continual, clean and concise feel to your site. The theme of each page of the website includes headers, layout, background and overall visual design. When picking a page layout, focus on the

clarity of the message being delivered. Choose images, graphics and fonts that are visually appealing.

Including media such as high-resolution photographs and video will keep your website current and provide a polished effect to your site. Select photos that complement the content of your webpages and not distract the reader from receiving the main message. Again be consistent with your rich media content across all your social media sites (LinkedIn, YouTube, Flickr). All websites need to be monitored and updated from time to time, but for some businesses, constant updates may not be relevant or necessary.

5. **Make Your Website Accessible:** Make your website accessible by choosing a domain name that is easy to remember and directly relates to the name of your company or message you are sending. For example, if your business is called SF Cupcakes, purchase and claim the domain "www.SFCupcakes.com". If the domain is something unrelated, visitors to your site will have a hard time finding your page and it may cause some confusion. Once the domain name has been chosen, the home or landing page needs to be consistent and identifiable with your brand so visitors are easily reminded whose website they are looking at.

6. **Have a "Call to Action":** A call to action on your site will engage the visitor to interact and make a decision. For example, a prompt that asks visitors to sign up for an email newsletter or hear about upcoming promotions and events. This is a great way to capture information from your visitors and build a network of people that are interested. If your services and/or products are labeled and promoted correctly on your site, visitors will want to participate in a call to action.

It is absolutely necessary that your company has a company website. Be sure to follow the guidelines above to maximize the appearance and accessibility of your website.

Writing a Blog

When writing a blog post the goal is to strongly convey your message across and ultimately gain readers. You do not have to be a professional writer to accomplish this. We have outlined 7 Steps for writing a successful blog post:

1. **Select the Right Subject:** Make a connection with your readers. Do this by providing them with information about something they want to learn how to do or a subject of interest. Readers will want to read more about topics that apply to their life.

2. **Grab Readers Attention with the Title:** The title is your first impression to readers. It needs to capture your reader's attention and state what the blog post is about.

3. **Keep Readers Attention with Opening Lines:** Now that you have captured your reader's attention, you must keep it. Follow up your title with an opening paragraph that summarizes what your blog post is about. Make this brief, but enticing.

4. **Use Keywords:** Be more conscious of the words you are using. By utilizing certain keywords, you will increase Search Engine Optimization (SEO) for your blog and website. Keep your readers focused on the main point of your post. These keywords will reinforce that point.

5. **Make the Blog an Appropriate Length:** Blogs with a high word count can be overwhelming for a reader. Writing a long blog can discourage readers from reading past the first couple of lines. A blog around 300 words is an appropriate length. If you feel the need to write more, make sure to use less than 1000 words.

6. **Use Lists/Headings:** Utilizing lists and headings helps readers to scan for a blog's key points. It is visually easier to read this type of format online rather than a traditional essay format.

7. **Conclude by Reinforcing a Call to Action:** Effectively convey your message to readers by reinforcing a call to action. This helps them to retain the message and proceed to the next step of action.

Writing a successful blog is easy when you reiterate a theme or message throughout the article. Pay attention to your content and use a reader friendly outline.

Now it's your turn to write one.

Website and Blog Checklist

- ❑ Is the domain/web address clearly branded and easily identifiable?

- ❑ Is the brand/purpose of the site readily seen on the home/landing page?

- ❑ Does the site include information about the business such as purpose, story, background or 'About Us'?

- ❑ Does the homepage contain links to other sites/pages/accounts such as Facebook, Twitter or other affiliate groups?

- ❑ Are there clear icons/links? Buttons for social media sites?

- ❑ Is contact information available such as email/phone/address?

- ❑ Call to Action - Are services/products labeled and promoted properly?

- ❑ Is there a medium to interact with clients such as an email newsletter signup?

- ❑ Does the theme of the website continue throughout each page?

- ❑ How are the graphics of the page? Images, fonts, layout, etc.

- ❑ How often is the website updated/monitored? Is it relevant?

What's Your Score?

Rate your business based upon the answers to the previous questions.

How Many You Have		Score
0	=	0
1-3	=	30
4-6	=	60
7-9	=	80
10+	=	90

Your Website & Blog Score = _____

Suggestions, Tips & Tools

Now that we know all the criteria needed to be met in order to have a well-rounded and fully functioning company website and blog, how do you choose which platform will host your site? There are multiple hosting sites where you can claim a domain address.

WordPress for Business

WordPress is a great platform to utilize to start your website. It is not just a platform for blogs anymore. Many companies have used it to create their entire website including a custom home page and a blog on a sub-page. 74.6 million sites depend on WordPress and in the realm of self-hosted sites, WordPress accounts for 18.9% of all websites.[5] This includes companies like CNN and People Magazine. Here is information and advice on how to utilize WordPress:

- WordPress allows you to create your own blog or website in minutes and its services are free. You have complete control of it and you have the ability to post as frequently as you would

5 *See the Reference section at the end of the book for further information and sources*

like. Anyone with a valid email address can use WordPress to create a blog or a website.

- Want your website to be as unique as your company? WordPress offers over 100 (even more with the paid premium service) of customizable designs to suit all kinds of personalities and content. From classically minimal to edgy and modern, there is something for everyone. Journalists, photographers, business owners; whoever you are, there is sure to be a design that suits everyone's needs.

- It is easy to include lots of creative, interactive content. If you already have media on other sites like YouTube, Flickr and SoundCloud, WordPress makes it easy to upload your photos, music and video to your site from those sources in a snap. You automatically get 3 gigabytes of storage space. That's equivalent to over 2,500 photo files or around 1,000 songs.

- WordPress will help drive traffic to your blog. By including tags with your posts, WordPress automatically adds them to their global tag system and tag surfer, so people who are interested in the topics you cover will easily be able to search for your content.

- The integrated stats system lets you view activity on your blog and find out more about who your audience is. How many people viewed your blog post? What links did they click on? Were they referred from another site? Find out what people are really reading so you can better attack your target market.

- If you find yourself wanting more, you can upgrade to WordPress premium services for even more storage, features and capabilities. Create a custom website with full control and custom features by visiting www.wordpress.org. Custom WordPress sites allow us to set up your site for a flat fee and there are no additional fees for space or upgraded features.

- If you don't need all the bells and whistles that a custom website offers, create a simple website or blog of your own in just minutes by visiting wordpress.com.

We work with our clients to create custom websites and blogs. These sites allow clients to have full control of their content and use all kinds of custom features. Developing a website is vital to creating a successful online presence.

Wix for Business

In today's technological society, there are lots of website building platforms that exist that are easily operated do-it-yourself (DIY) websites like Wix. It is easy to maneuver and only takes about 10 minutes to personalize. Wix is a free service tool that allows users to create their own customized website. The foremost benefit of using Wix is that there is no coding involved. It's simple, easy and Google friendly. Here are a few benefits of using Wix:

- It is a free, secure and reliable service
- Hundreds of website design templates to choose from which will make your website unique and exciting
- Attracts more traffic to your site through Google, Yahoo and Bing
- Compatible with top mobile apps, Facebook, Twitter and blogs
- Creates an opportunity to generate your own online store

As you can see, Wix is a useful tool not only in creating the foundation of your business but in its maintenance and growth. At its most basic level, Wix provides a platform in which to create your own unique and customized website through easy and simple instruction. In addition to the free plan, Wix provides premium plans which include free hosting, Google analytics, premium support, your own domain, storage and bandwidth. Ranging from $5 to $20 a month, these upgraded plans grant certain benefits that are optimal for personal use, entrepreneurs, freelancers and ecommerce.

There are other hosted website companies similar to Wix such as Weebly and Squarespace. Depending on your industry and goals select which platform is best for your business.

Monitoring and Measuring – Alexa

Want to find out how to track your web traffic data? Alexa.com is a free service that can provide you with web traffic reporting by collecting and analyzing data on browsing behavior. In the world of web analytics, Alexa.com is a leading contributor in Internet optimization. Alexa.com is a subsidiary of the popular online marketplace, Amazon, that collects user data through Explorer, Firefox and Google Chrome Internet browsers, as well as through various extensions that users download. These extensions and toolbars collect data on a users' browsing habits and preferences in exchange for providing helpful tips about websites. Users can find out how popular a website is or see similar sites and analytics related to a website's traffic. Alexa.com offers many benefits for small businesses and large organizations to enhance their understanding of their consumers, their competitors and consumer behavior.

Alexa.com offers businesses unique tools and services to improve how they communicate their product or service offerings through their website's Search Engine Optimization (SEO). For example, Alexa.com can analyze a business' website to assess language used and suggest more effective keywords to take advantage of on the website using the Keyword Difficulty Tool. The Competitor Keyword Matrix will determine what keywords a business's competitor is using on their site, enabling companies to ensure they are not missing out on potential consumers that are being targeted by their competitors.

Alexa.com also enhances marketing by providing research and analytics on a business's target market, providing clients with information on related websites that their potential consumers are visiting. This allows a business to post blog articles on these related fields, or to partner with some of these organizations to promote their shared interest.

Alexa.com maintains extensive data on hundreds of thousands of websites worldwide which enables them to provide information and analytics to any business that is interested, including smaller businesses such as restaurants, law firms, engineering firms, auto body shops and large firms such as oil and gas companies, franchises, and more. Alexa.com offers seven-day free trials for many of their tools and analytics. In a world where SEO makes up a significant portion of your passive marketing (PM) strategy, Alexa's Internet tools can be a worthwhile investment to bolster marketing and business development strategies.

Monitoring and Measuring - Google Analytics

Do you want a better understanding of the customer experience? Google Analytics makes it simple and easy to track your customer's experience by bridging customer behavior, site performance, and more across all your online platforms. The digital analytics you are provided with gives you insight on how to make the data work for you and drive real impact. Ultimately, it allows you to measure the impact your website has on its users and your business. Google Analytics provides support for businesses of all sizes, helping them to see what is working and what needs improvement.

For a complete view of the customer experience, Google Analytics 360 is available to purchase. Google Analytics 360 provides advanced solutions, services, and support for large enterprises. It helps understand people and their behaviors so that your business can provide value service and experience when the users need it the most. Equipped with cutting-edge intelligence, the 360 Suite uses Google's machine learning capabilities that allows you to see users that are likely to convert, customers with high revenue potential, and other relevant and actionable business insights.

Google Analytics 360 comes equipped with comprehensive administrative capabilities that gives more oversight when it comes to user management, auditing, and account permissions. It also provides you and your team real-time data snapshots of key metrics across all products. Having all the integrations the 360 Suite has to offer at your accessibility, you have quick access to data the saves you time and increases your teams efficiency.

Combining enterprise analytics, tagging, site optimization, data visualization, market research, attribution, and audience management, Google Analytics 360 gives businesses a powerful measurement solution. Its seven measurement solutions are designed to give a seamless user experience, using cross-product data integration to help your enterprise gain useful insights and drive better results daily.

CHAPTER 8
KEY 2
ONLINE DIRECTORIES

"We cannot limit ourselves to continuing on the path we have already opened."

— Amancio Ortega, Founder, Zara

A<small>N ONLINE DIRECTORY</small> is a web tool that searches and groups information for the user's convenience. An online directory assists users in finding what they need online and are considered a reliable go-to source for finding businesses, products or services. Online directories are the most common way people search for additional information on a company. Therefore, it is important that you have optimized your business's search results to let customers learn about you and ultimately drive your business.

Examples of Online Directories

Google My Business, Google Maps, Yahoo! Local, Yellow Pages, Bing, Yelp, CitySearch, Angie's List

Benefits of an Online Directory

Online directories managed efficiently have many benefits including:

- **Increased exposure** - Others can easily find you. Search yourself - what do others find when they search for your business? It is crucial that your business is easy to find online.

- **Scoping out the competition** - Look for similar businesses. Be sure to see how your online presence compares to your competitors.

- **Information access to your consumer** - You can display current and correct contact information. This includes your location, phone number, hours of operation and more. It makes information easily attainable to your customer.

> *Key Learning* - Focus on optimizing your search result listing, distinguishing your business from competitors, making your business easy to find, using rich media and monitoring and updating your Internet presence.

Online Directory Strategies

Online directories are popular platforms for individuals to use when trying to find information, therefore, developing your business online directories is important for creating brand awareness and customer satisfaction. The following strategies can help your business progress it's online directory presence:

1. **Optimize Your Search Results Listing:** When a search is done on your business, are you the first listing that pops up? If not, are you on the first page? If not, review the online presence of your business and see what is keeping it from showing up in searches. Although you may appear on the search list, it is important to

optimize your appearance so your business will show up when you need it to. What are the results when you search for your business name in Google search? If results are minimal or your business does not show up, something needs to be changed to get your business to appear in the search.

Consider the following options when searching for your business online:

- "Type of Service" search
- Similar business name search
- Keywords related to your business
- Location-based searches

It is important to consider how specific the search needs to be in order to wield the correct results. If you are a sushi restaurant in Walnut Creek and search for "Walnut Creek Sushi" and "Sushi Bay Area", will your business be included in the results?

If your business is first on the search list, great. Confirm that your listing includes the correct and current business information including contact information, business hours, photos and the link to your website. Keep in mind that if your business is not listed... Someone else is.

There are a number of different online directories that can be used to search for businesses. Search for yours on mainstream directories (Google, Bing, Yahoo!, Yelp) as well as specialized directories that are more tailored to your industry.

Search Engine Optimization (SEO)

- Helps drive traffic to your site
- Off-page SEO (work that takes place separate from your website)
- On-page SEO (website changes to increase rank)

2. **Differentiate Your Business from Others:** Take note of similar businesses that appear in the search results for your business. If the business names are similar, think about a way of repositioning your business to differentiate it from the rest.

3. **Make Your Business Easy to Find:** How easy is it to find your business when searching? Search Google for your business and see where your business appears. You want your business name and website to appear first before any secondary related articles. This way users are guided to your website, which is the voice on what your business is and what it offers. Having a domain/web address that is clearly branded and easily identifiable to your business will result in a more accurate search. For Search Engine Optimization (SEO), consider the results when you search the services offered with a location in the search engine. Make sure your business appears with the right combination of keywords.

4. **Use Online Advertisements:** Create an advertisement that will appear on search engines. An advertisement will benefit your business by creating brand awareness and also attract customers to your business. Using Google Ads is a great way to track the traffic to your business and you will only have to pay if people click your ads using Google.

5. **Use Rich Media:** It is a good idea for photos and videos to be present when your business appears in a search result. Photos and videos are more interesting than text. They are current and interactive with your online audience and will attract more attention to your business. It goes without saying that your photos and videos need to be relevant in content to your business and of good quality. Using YouTube or Flickr will also boost your presence in searches. Seeing photos and videos in search results can be achieved by using key terms in naming your photo and video files.

6. **Monitor and Update Internet Presence:** Regularly monitor your internet presence. Search results on your business need to be both current and relevant. Recent activities will show up higher in

search results, so having your Twitter, Facebook, news and events on your website help keep your business active and current.

Online Directory Checklist

- ❑ Is your business on Google Local/Maps, Yahoo Local, Yellow Pages, etc.?
- ❑ Does the business name appear in a Google search? What page of the search results?
- ❑ How specific is the search in order to yield the correct results?
- ❑ Does the business location appear in Google Maps?
- ❑ Does the business appear in Yahoo Local?
- ❑ SEO - When you search the services offered with location in Google does the company appear within the map and listed below?
- ❑ Does the business appear higher on directories than similar business names in the results of a Google search?
- ❑ Do listings of the business contain the correct information?
- ❑ Are there any photos in a Google Image search?
- ❑ Are there directions to the business?
- ❑ Are business hours listed?
- ❑ Is there any other information about the business provided?

What's Your Score?

Rate your business based upon the answers to the previous questions.

How Many You Have		Score
0	=	0
1-3	=	30
4-6	=	60
7-9	=	80
10+	=	90

Your Online Directory Score = _____

Suggestions, Tips & Tools

Now you know how to optimize your company on online directories to ensure the best possible search results. The following are helpful tips on how to maximize your business in current online directories.

Google My Business

Search engines use information it receives on businesses from multiple sources. Your business will probably already be listed in Google, but Google My Business is a free business listing that allows you to control what information Google has and presents that information to people who are searching for your business. It allows for business owners and people to upload photos, write reviews, share hours of operation, add categories (search terms) so people can find your business and offer discounts and promotions. Google My Business also allows for you to engage with consumers and get insights about your company.

If you have not listed your business on Google My Business, chances are that Google has already listed you. To verify your listing, go to Google My Business and claim your company. Once you do that, Google will either call you or send you a letter to verify that the business is actually yours. After you have been verified, you can update the details of your business listing. Ask returning customers to leave positive reviews for your business because the more your business is rated, the higher your business will appear in the rankings.

Google Maps for Business

This is a free mapping service that will give directions to your business. It even offers a street view, which can show actual exterior pictures of almost any address. If you are listed, your business location will appear in a Google Maps search. A lot of people use the GPS on their phone to locate places. Being listed on Google Maps is very helpful for customers coming to your business.

If someone searches "gas stations" in Google Maps, they will find different gas stations around them. Depending on how zoomed in the map is, they may find around twenty gas stations. Having a good ranking in Google Places will help your business make it to the first, larger map that pops up on Google Maps.

Yahoo! Local for Business

Yahoo Local is an information portal that provides business reviews, top rated services and events that are local to your area. If your business is not on Yahoo Local, you can submit a basic listing (free of cost) that will display your contact information, location, store hours, website, photo and the products and services your business offers.

CHAPTER 9
KEY 3
REVIEW SITES

"Make a customer, not a sale."
— *Katherine Barchetti, Founder, K. Barchetti Shops*

REVIEW SITES ON the web are available for users to post about their experiences regarding people, businesses, products or services. The use of review sites is considered a go-to for finding businesses and services. Having your business listed on review sites will increase your Search Engine Optimization (SEO). Review sites are one of the least understood, and therefore most intimidating areas of online marketing. Just because they provide a platform and community for your customers, does not mean they are not also a place you can have a voice as well. In fact, it is the opposite.

On review sites like Yelp, it is important to understand that 85% of Yelp reviews are 4-5 stars. By claiming or setting up your business on Yelp, when/if someone does write a bad review—you will be notified. If you do not set it up, and someone writes something bad about you—you have no idea it exists. By setting your business up on review sites, especially Yelp, you can take control of your brand and business. Ian Mitroff (1987) explains in his article titled *Effective Crisis Management*, "While planning cannot prevent every crisis, the process of planning teaches an organization how to cope more effectively with whatever does occur". Ian Mitroff goes on to state that, "In fact, a cardinal rule of crisis management is that no crisis ever unfolds exactly as it was envisioned or planned for. For this reason, effective crisis management is a never-ending process, not an event with a beginning and an end." Setting up your business on Yelp enables you to manage a crisis, such as bad reviews, that may effect your brand reputation.

If someone writes something good, great, however if someone writes something bad, you can flag it because you are the owner of it. By having your Yelp profile set up correctly, it is going to increase the likelihood that people write positive reviews because you are going to be able to brand yourself and promote yourself in a positive way. The other benefit would be that if someone does write a one-star review and they talk about how horrible you are, (especially if they are obviously crazy) then it is okay (not great, but okay) because then another person is going to see that one-star review and go "Wow, I identify with that one-star review." And then that means another crazy person is not going to contact you or come to your business. If you have 50 five-star reviews, and 1 crazy one, leave it because there are people who identify with the crazy person, and they won't come. This is perfect because you do not want those crazy people coming to your business anyways.

The most important part of this equation is claiming your review site so that you have ownership and control over how people perceive your business. Claiming also allows you to add three categories to your Yelp. Normally people only have one category, but yelp allows you to have three for free, which when optimized can help you show up better on Yelp and on Google because you have been identified for more categories.

Examples of Review Sites

Yelp, Angie's List, Google Reviews/Zagat, Amazon, TripAdvisor

Benefits of a Review Site

Review sites use user-generated content. This is content that your audience creates about your company. Productively managing your company on review sites will help boost your company. Here are reasons why review sites are so useful:

- Consumers view this as a trustworthy source of information in comparison to other forms of media - Review sites rely on word of mouth. People trust personal accounts more than advertisements.

- Companies can offer additional information to consumers - Review sites allow businesses to add a wealth of supplemental components to their listing. For example, advertising special offers/coupons.

- Ability to interact with consumers - You can respond to reviews and use these sites as a forum to thank those who provide feedback.

- Learn from negative reviews - If someone writes something bad about your company on a review site, it allows you to avoid making the same mistake twice.

Key Learning - Focus on claiming your listing, dealing with negative reviews and trends, creating promotions and monitoring your traffic.

Using Review Sites to Your Advantage

Review sites can be tricky because you are not in control of the comments and feedback you get from customers. However, you are in control of how you respond to the feedback. Here are some way to take advantage of review sites to maximize your business potential:

1. **Claim your business page:** Often times, your business may be listed before you have had a chance to register it yourself. Take control of your page and claim your listing to allow your business to communicate and interact with customers as well as respond to reviewers. When you are effectively managing your business page, make sure your listing has accurate and updated information (photos, directions, business hours, contact information, etc.). Remember: if you are not listed, then it is highly likely that your competitors are.

   If you have not claimed your page yet, doing so is easy. Search for your business on the review site of your choice and click on your profile. Somewhere on that page you will find a link that will have some variation of the question 'Is this your business?' Click that link to authorize yourself as the business owner. Once you have claimed your page, keep your business information up to date and accurate so customers know the page is current.

   The benefits that come with claiming your business include:

   - Full control of your page
   - Accuracy of business information
   - Reliable sources and information
   - Ability to respond to reviews and comments
   - Monitor traffic and visitor statistics
   - Keep customers up to date with offers (check-in, discounts, etc.)

2. **Dealing with negative reviews and trends:** Negative reviews are inevitable. How you deal with them will make a positive or negative impression on you and your business. It is important to acknowledge any bad review by responding to the customer in an effort to try to resolve the situation. Often times you will discover that a bad review can be turned into a good one by simply apologizing for the bad experience, being honest about how the mistake was made and sharing the efforts you have made to improve the situation.

In some cases, reviews that are entirely false can be made, in turn reflecting poorly on your business. In these situations, a response is necessary to explain in a professional manner why the review is false in an effort to discredit the false review.

3. **Promotions:** Customers are happy when they come across a good deal. Bring attention to your site by offering a promotion. Create a promotion by offering customers an additional bonus by visiting your review site. Customers are more likely give your business a try and are also more likely to return to your site when they know promotions have been offered in the past.

   For example, when using Yelp, you can create a "check-in offer" where customers can receive a deal or discount simply by logging in on your Yelp page when they are at your place of business.

4. **Monitoring traffic:** Once you have gained complete access to your business page, do not forget to monitor the traffic and keep the page current by updating it often. Respond to the reviews listed on your page. Let customers know that you are thankful for their feedback and that they are encouraged to leave any tips or recommendations they want to offer to both your business and other viewers. When it comes to negative reviews, attempt to clear up any issues that may be presented and remind viewers that you appreciate their business.

   Keep track of the increase or decrease in the number of viewers. If you receive more visits after you have updated your page or offered a promotion, you can see the results in page views.

Review Site Checklist

- ☐ Is the business listed in places like Yelp, Google Local, etc.?
- ☐ Is business information provided?
- ☐ Are there photos?
- ☐ How many reviews are given?
- ☐ What's the average review score?

❑ Does a search of services offered yield the business within Yelp?

❑ Are there any special offers or promotions available?

❑ Does the business appear on any other online review sites?

❑ Are there sufficient reviews on those sites?

❑ Has the business been reviewed by any industry specific critics or websites?

What's Your Score?

Rate your business based upon the answers to the previous questions.

How Many You Have		Score
0	=	0
1-3	=	30
4-6	=	60
7-9	=	80
10+	=	90

Your Review Sites Score = _____

Suggestions, Tips & Tools

Now you know the criterion that helps to maintain a thriving business on review sites. Make sure that you regulate these accounts frequently.

Yelp for Business

As of June 2016, Yelp has 23 million average monthly mobile app unique users, 69 million average monthly mobile web unique visitors and 73 million average monthly desktop unique visitors.[6] Yelp is a widely used review site that provides a great way for customers to learn more about your business and what your business has to offer. It is free to join, easy to set up and allows you to provide users with current information and the ability for users to give feedback on your business. Once you have set up a Yelp account, how can you optimize the results of your business showing up when it is searched?

- Run a test search for your business name and see if it appears

- Search for specific key terms that yield the correct results and see if the search provides links to your main website

- Multiple types of services listed for your business, check-in offers and a high rating will improve the search results for your business

Google Reviews & Zagat for Business

For businesses to increase their revenues and have strong brand awareness, they must critically assess their online presence and monitor their pages and information on review sites. A great starting point for companies to enhance their brand awareness is through Google. Google My Business allows any type of business, whether you own a Korean Restaurant, a Corporate Law Firm, or a Fitness franchise, to maintain location and contact information, hours of operation, average busy times and more on a Google Page. Perhaps the most valuable tool available to businesses through Google pages are customer reviews. Customers are able to leave a review of your business based on a 5 point Likert scale while also leaving comments that describe their experience. Here are three tips and tricks for using Google Reviews and Zagat (which was acquired by Google) to enhance your business:

---

6 See the Reference section at the end of the book for further information and sources

- **Respond to Customers:** The Google Review platform allows you to read and respond to customer comments allowing you to build rapport with your customer base. If a repeat patron to your restaurant leaves a glowing review, you can respond to them with a personalized 'thank you'. If a new customer had a bad experience, you can offer to make it up to them with a discount or ask them to contact you to get more information. Not only will these interactions improve your customers' experience, it will allow potential customers to see how engaged you are with your consumer base and will positively influence your reputation. Remember to be brief to save both you and the customer time.

- **Ask for Reviews:** You can quickly and easily ask customers to review your business on Google or Zagat. Place a link on your webpage that takes customers to your pages, remind them as they leave your restaurant, or suggest to potential new clients that they check out your reviews on these sites. The comments should be unbiased, so we do not recommend you offer deals or discounts in exchange for a review. Word of mouth is a powerful way to enhance your existing reputation and word can easily spread that you are compensating for positive reviews.

- **Use Zagat for Restaurants:** In 2011, Google purchased Zagat (www.zagat.com), a renowned restaurant review source, and aligned it with Google for business. Zagat allows users to review the quality of food, décor and service for restaurants in many U.S. cities. Users evaluate the restaurant on a 5-point scale in each of these three categories. Comments on the restaurant are aggregated into one description using the most commented keywords or phrases. You can showcase your menu, add photos of plated meals or the location to tempt customers and manage reservations through your OpenTable account through Zagat. All the information maintained by Zagat is managed through a restaurant's Google Page, making it easy to update your information on both sites through one platform.

- **Maintain Accuracy**: While monitoring your Google or Zagat review pages, you may notice that a reviewer has mistakenly assigned a review to your page that is not reviewing your business but a neighboring business or one with a similar name. You are able to flag inaccurate or inappropriate information and reviews for possible removal by Google. This allows you to ensure that the reviews posted on Google are accurate. We recommend that you only use this feature when there is a factual error in a review, otherwise you compromise the accurate and sincere nature of customer reviews. Take negative feedback as an opportunity to review business practices and only make changes as required.

Google and Zagat reviews are excellent ways to take advantage of the most powerful form of marketing: word of mouth. By encouraging accurate and honest reviews, Google gives businesses and restaurants methods to receive feedback they otherwise would not see with traditional word-of-mouth marketing.

CHAPTER 10
KEY 4
ONLINE SOCIAL NETWORKS

"Social media is changing the way we communicate and the way we are perceived, both positively and negatively. Every time you post a photo, or update your status, you are contributing to your own digital footprint and personal brand."

- Amy Jo Martin, Author, Speaker, Entrepreneur, Founder & CEO of Digital Royalty

MAKING YOUR BUSINESS a part of social networks is crucial to your success in increasing brand awareness and sales opportunities. Social networks are hubs of information that have constant updates and opinions on your business. These social networking sites are new tools that have changed the shape of small business marketing. Monitor the content on these social sites to keep your business's image in your favor. The advantages of having your business on social networks include connecting with peers, communication through forums and inclusion in a professional community.

Examples of Social Networks

Facebook, LinkedIn, Google+

Benefits of a Social Network

Social networks are a great way to connect and interact with your target market and prospective customers. Using social networks helps a company by:

- Creating open communication with customers – Be involved in the conversation with those following you or talking to you through social networks.

- Ability to connect and network – Associate your business with related pages and people to gain a larger network and build your connections.

- Establishing a following – Invite past customers to view your page and be active on your social networks to encourage new customers.

- Keeping our company at the front of mind - By making the content interesting and enticing, it gives people a reason to visit your page and to be thinking about your company.

Key Learning - Focus on creating and actively monitoring your business page, being active, branding your presence, adding starter content, expanding your network, social media blunders and generating new leads.

Promoting Your Business on Social Networks

Social networks can be utilized for business purposes if they are effectively and efficiently monitored. The content you put on these social sites about your business will help to develop brand awareness and can help create a positive image.

1. **Create and monitor your social networks:** With your social networks, you can have multiple tabs of information, list basic information, post regular updates and expand your following.

   If you do not have an account on any social network, get started by claiming your business page. A business page is different than a personal profile. A business page gives you the ability to gain and recruit fans.

   Your business profile needs to contain the following:

   • Description of your business, products and services

   • Appealing visual content – photos, videos, comments

   • Contact information

   • Website URL

   • Invitation for visitors to join your mailing list

   • Public setting that enables customers and prospects to find you easily

2. **Be active:** Once you have an account, keep it active by participating on the site. Write articles that interest your community and bring traffic to your site, send messages, start and join groups, introduce people and send referrals. The more involved you are, the more you will be seen as an expert in your area. Remember to keep your business pages professional across all sites. Just because some social networks are used casually and for personal use does not mean your page has to be. Whether it is the newest social media, rising technology, or latest mainstream news, do not be blind to change. Keep your business cutting edge so you do not get overlooked because other businesses have chosen to be more forward, more progressive, and more active within their community.

3. **Brand your presence:** Upload your logo, pictures and background across all of your business pages. This will help establish credibility and build brand awareness.

4. **Add starter content:** Need ideas on what content to have on your business page? Start by announcing upcoming events, join in on hot conversation topics or answer questions asked by your customers, share information and give and receive tips and practical advice that applies to your business. You can also try partnering with a nonprofit business to do any of the items just listed. The idea is to keep people engaged and interested in visiting your page.

    Another thing you can do when uploading content to your business page is to share web links in your posts. This can be done by posting polls and surveys, linking event homepages and registration pages, archived email marketing newsletters, adding blogs (yours and others), including websites (yours and others in your area of expertise) and relevant videos, photos or podcasts.

5. **Expand Your Network:** There are a number of methods you can use to expand your network. For example, one way is to send an invitation to join your email list. Another idea is to add interactive social icons to the following:

    - Website

    - Email campaigns (in a sidebar, in the footer)

    - Outgoing email signature

    - Business Card

    - Printed collateral: mailers, flyers, invoices, etc.

    More ways to expand your network include putting up signage in your storefront window, adding a message to your voicemail and including a note on point-of-sale receipts and house coupons.

6. **Social Media Blunders:** There are a few guidelines that are best to be followed when posting updates to your business pages on social networks. These simple guidelines will help you to maximize

your social network and minimize the potential of irritating your followers.

What Not to Do with Your Social Networks:

- No pitching

- Try not to overly self-promote

- Don't offer incentives to get reviews or sharing

- Typically avoid personal information, politics, sports, religion, etc.

Social Media Pitfalls

It is important to remember to post appropriate content on all your social media sites because you never know who will have access to it. Kids these days are very social media savvy and everything goes viral. Donna Mitroff (2012) was the head of broadcasting for a top TV network and explains in her book *Fables and the Art of Leadership* that she had "the responsibility for insuring that the content of children's TV programs was not only age appropriate, but also actually aided children's health and development." In the same way, you want to regulate all your content, making sure it is appropriate for all audiences who come across your sites such as your website, blog, Facebook, Twitter, etc. People are impressionable and your brand's reputation is on the line, therefore, you want to put the best of your brand out to the world.

Social Networks Checklist

- ❑ Does the business have a Facebook account?

- ❑ Is the information presented within a Facebook PAGE and not a profile?

- ❑ Is basic business information listed?

- ❑ Does the Facebook page have information and pictures of the business?

❑ How many followers does the page have?

❑ Is the page regularly updated?

❑ Does the business have a LinkedIn account?

❑ Is the information provided up to date?

❑ Is the business connected with other social media accounts?

❑ Are there credible recommendations and endorsements provided on LinkedIn?

What's Your Score?

Rate your business based upon the answers to the previous questions.

How Many You Have		Score
0	=	0
1-3	=	30
4-6	=	60
7-9	=	80
10+	=	90

Your Social Networks Score = _____

Suggestions, Tips & Tools

Now that you know the key points and best practices for using social networks for business, we can view specific social networks and learn how to optimize your business results on them.

Facebook for Business

Facebook is the most popular social network used today. For June 2016, Facebook had an average of 1.13 billion daily active users and 1.71 billion monthly active users.[7] With more than a billion active users, Facebook is a great place to start when creating a business page. With a Facebook business page, you can have multiple pages of information, basic information listed, the ability to post regular updates and expand your following. If you do not have an account on Facebook yet, get started by claiming your business page. A business page is different than a personal profile. A business page gives you the ability to gain and recruit fans.

Facebook is currently the top social networking site with the most monthly visitors in comparison to other platforms. Due to this, it has become an important free mechanism to market and promote business. Here are the top 5 reasons why Facebook is a good marketing tool for business:

1. **Business Newsfeed:** Facebook Business Pages provide a space to showcase new products, promotions and upcoming events to your followers. By consistently providing fresh and varied content (like a combination of photos, videos, promotions, business updates, etc.) it gives reasons for followers to return.

2. **Communication Channel Between Business and Fans:** Having a business page allows for a two-way communication between a company and its followers. Anyone can comment on posts and provide feedback on products, while the company is able to provide customer service if questions or concerns arise. This helps build and maintain relationships.

3. **Word of Mouth Marketing:** Every time the content on your page or the page itself is shared or liked by someone, or when a customer checks in at your business location, the link to the content is reposted on that person's Facebook wall and newsfeed for all their friends to see. The increased exposure of your Business

---

7 *See the Reference section at the end of the book for further information and sources*

Page can result in an increase of brand awareness and can generate interest and attract new customers.

4. **Search Engine Optimization Opportunities:** Having a Facebook Business Page can aid in improving your SEO score, particularly when you do things like use a custom Facebook URL and put relevant keywords and links in the "About" and "Info" sections of your business page.

5. **Analytics Tools to Track Your Progress:** Facebook has a free Page Insights feature, which provides useful information, such as the demographic of your audience, how many times you have been mentioned in someone's post, what tabs generate the most interest, where the referrals to your page are coming from and number of times your post and page were viewed during a certain period. This information helps you assess and change your content strategy to make Facebook a more effective marketing tool.

The benefits of using Facebook for business are clear. It provides a great opportunity to grow your business, not only by allowing you to market it and create a community around it, but also by helping you analyze and improve your strategy.

LinkedIn for Business

As the leading professional networking site in the world, LinkedIn has transformed the traditional process of recruitment and job search. Recruiters largely use LinkedIn to buy access to data about LinkedIn users for hiring purposes. Job seekers use this space to connect with mentors, employers, coworkers, peers and influencers. On a daily basis, companies and contributors post advice columns, the latest news about the company, and other interesting finds. LinkedIn is driven by trusted relationships and two-way agreements, meaning that employees are now directly associated with employers online, but you can also demonstrate collaborating and provide individual and company references for the public to see. Not only does LinkedIn tailor your home page news feed to your interests, LinkedIn also creates a sense of community by notifying your connections to congratulate you on your new job, anniversaries, or other notable moments. This large, successful and rapidly growing social networking platform is one that will continue to shape the world we live in today.

You can use LinkedIn to elevate your company by doing specific things that will optimize your business in searches, therefore creating new leads and more hires. LinkedIn seeks to establish professional relationships and build professional networks. Your LinkedIn profile is the best place to showcase your greatest successes and future aspirations. Show off your skills, highlight your experiences and identify your goals. Your LinkedIn profile should help you show up in searches for the right people at the right time. Here are tips that will help you to develop a LinkedIn profile that is eye-catching and makes you stand out among others:

- **Have a Professional Profile Photo:** Make your picture a simple, professional headshot. Not a "selfie" you took on your own. People remember faces more than they remember names. This is the first impression you make to the public.

- **Make Your Headline Attract Attention:** Keep your headline short. Do not just list your job title in the headline. Include keywords that your particular audience would search for to make your profile more findable.

- **Develop an "Elevator Pitch" Summary:** Beyond the headline, the first few sentences of your summary are key because this is what hooks the attention of those looking at your profile. An "elevator pitch" is what you would tell a future employer if you were in an elevator with them and had only 60 seconds to pitch yourself or your business. It is meant to be enthralling. In this section, list three to five key skills, goals or accomplishments that you bring to the table or have attained. You can include photos, videos or infographics of your work to make your summary section more enticing.

- **Have a Complete Profile:** To make your LinkedIn profile complete, list your industry and location, an up-to-date position, two past positions, education, skills, a profile photo and have at least 50 connections (ideally "500+" connections). This is important because users with fully complete profiles are 40 times more likely to receive opportunities through LinkedIn.[8]

One of the amazing tools of LinkedIn is their article publishing. LinkedIn long-form publishing serves as a platform for members to contribute professional insights and expertise to the public. This simple and easy tool allows users to learn from others in the profession and enables users to establish their own professional identity by expressing their opinions and sharing their experiences. Here are five tips on publishing a successful LinkedIn article of short post:

1. **Talk about something you know:** Having expertise in a subject draws people's attention and makes them want to hear what you have to say and take advice from you. Maybe you took on a challenge and were able to overcome it. Tell them how you did it. Maybe you experienced failure and learned something from that experience. Let them know about that too. Or maybe you want to talk about a problem that your industry is currently facing. Share with the reader some possible solutions.

2. **Be authentic:** Authenticity is more valuable than eloquent words that fit nicely together. Having a genuine voice will distinguish you from a generic post. When you speak with authenticity, your words mean so much more because they bring out your passion. An authentic voice is relatable and credible. Your words have value when you tell the truth and believe in what you are writing about.

3. **Be focused and concise:** Be sure that your posts are not super lengthy. It simply needs to be detailed enough to cover the main points in an organized and concise manner, no more and no less.

4. **Make sure what you post is appropriate**: Whatever your post may be about, make sure it is appropriate. This is your chance to establish your professional identity, so you want people to respect your opinions. You want to build credibility with these posts and be able to positively influence other LinkedIn users, not

---

8 *See the Reference section at the end of the book for further information and sources*

tarnish your image. For example, if you write about a subject with heavy political influence, be cautious about the words you use. Although you want to express your opinions, you do not want to go overboard and aggravate readers.

5. **Visuals matter:** Upload pictures, videos, and other documents into your post to engage your readers. Visuals help to establish concrete examples and share information in ways that words cannot. Sometimes when there are too many words on a page, it becomes overwhelming. Space your thoughts out by including visual relief.

LinkedIn is much more than just creating a profile. Rather, it is a tool to engage with your network, allowing you to tap into your alumni networks, follow your favorite companies, post or share relevant articles, research job opportunities, and reach out to recruiters. Take advantage of LinkedIn.

Google+ For Business

Google is the most common search engine in the world. Learning how to utilize it for your business is imperative for your online success. In urban cities, businesses and nightlife are constantly multiplying. To distinguish your business, it is important to utilize online social platforms.

Signing up with Google+ will put your business on the map. Whenever someone searches your company's name, they will be provided with your business' contact information, location, hours of service and any other information you choose to release. Anyone who searches for your company's name or any keywords associated with it will be able to find all the information they need quickly and easily. When searched, your company's profile will appear on the right side of the search results screen. Some other things you can do include:

- Consistently update your company's information - Your business is constantly changing and growing. Google allows your business the flexibility to update your online media influence and keep your consumers in the loop.

- Establish your company's image - You create the image for your company exactly the way you want it. You can post photos and updates to shape your online appearance and express your company's unique personality.

- Take advantage of Google Ads - You can choose to purchase advertising through Google, the largest search and most used engine in the world. This is a great way to expand your clientele.

- Invite customers to Google Hangouts - This is a fun way to connect with your customers and answer their personal questions or concerns. Additionally, you can provide an inside look into the behind-the-scenes workings of your business.

- Connect with other businesses and organizations - Stay connected with other companies, businesses and entrepreneurs by keeping them in your Circles on Google+. This allows you to stay up to date with the happenings of other groups or events taking place around your area.

CHAPTER 11
KEY 5
MICROBLOGGING

"The most dangerous thing for a branded product is low interest."

– Dietrich Mateschitz, Co-founder, Red Bull

T HE OAKLAND DIOCESE, (which is responsible for all of the Catholic churches, schools, and Catholics in general for all of Alameda County and Contra Costa County) was a consulting client of mine for three years, my work was focused on non-religious projects in nature (promoting events, and setting up Facebook and LinkedIn, etc.). When Pope Francis came in, they realized that I could help them with religious projects as well, using different social media tools. Especially when Pope Francis started taking selfies and using Instagram, Twitter, and such. At that time they asked me to do a workshop for 160 priests, at which point Microblogging was one of the biggest areas for them because that is what Pope Francis saw as reaching the masses. What I did live with the 160 priests was create a Twitter account. Twitter in particular is the classic form of microblogging; it's fast, easy, and quick. To set up a Twitter account literally takes at most five minutes. So I did it live, and went to Twitter.com and clicked "set up account" and you create a profile. It is simple, fast, and easy to do. So when it starts out, it asks you to follow somebody, so naturally we follow Britney Spears and MC Hammer before we finally get to the Pope. Then you can sync it with your other platforms and never need to go on it again, because whenever you post on Facebook or LinkedIn, it will automatically post to Twitter. That leads to more opportunities, more backlinks to your website, and boosts your Search Engine Optimization. Some people love microblogging, and some people do not use it that much, but ultimately it does not hurt to be on it, as it helps build your brand and grow your business.

Microblogging is one of the most efficient ways to share the latest news and updates. Microblogging sites are useful for interacting with followers and sharing the most current daily events. It is also a convenient tool for reminding followers about upcoming events and "front-of-mind" advertising by promoting and updating information leading up to an event. You can also use micro blogging to reach out to new customers through friends or friends of friends.

Microblogging is a broadcast medium in the form of blogging. It allows users to exchange small elements of content such as short sentences, individual images and/or video links. You can post about topics ranging from the simple, such as "what I'm doing right now," to the thematic, such as "sports cars." Commercial micro blogs also exist, to promote websites, services and/or products and to promote collaboration within an organization. Different micro blogging services offer features such as privacy settings, which allow users to control who can read their microblogs or alternative ways of publishing entries besides the web-based interface. These may include text messaging, instant messaging, e-mail, digital audio or digital video.

Examples of Micro-Blogging Platforms

Twitter, Tumblr, Instagram, Snapchat, Pintrest

Benefits of Microblogging

A microblog differs from a traditional blog because its content is typically smaller in both actual and aggregate file size. A company can use microblog platforms to:

- Interact online with daily events - Communicate with followers and fans by posting about current events and happenings.

- Remind followers about upcoming events and promotions - Utilize "front-of-mind" advertising techniques by promoting and updating information leading up to an event.

- Invite new customers – Attract followers, friends of your friends or use targeted user searches.

Key Learning - Focus on relating your business to current events. How can you relate to what is happening in the news or in your area? Remind everyone about upcoming events (whether it is yours or other local related events). Invite people to visit your website or business. Remember friends of friends can be potential customers who may also see your posts through micro-blogging.

Best Practices for Microblogging

With the fast-paced nature of social media, businesses may be unsure of how much to engage with customers through social media platforms. Businesses all struggle with the same reality: how much do I post and when?

Microblogging can be a fantastic tool for businesses to use to increase their marketplace presence. Microblogging is the practice of regularly posting short messages. This strategy enhances online presence, provides a method for directly communicating with your customers and allows you to have real time dialogue with a wide audience. Organizations that know Active Marketing (AM)/Passive Marketing (PM) techniques know that social media is a workhorse of marketing, helping engage potential customers both day and night. However, some businesses might not be aware that small changes in their current practices can allow them to take advantage of microblogging and see brand awareness and revenues grow. To get the most out of microblogging for your business, here are four tips:

1. **Short messages:** Microblogging uses quick and short messages to engage an audience. Businesses can ask a question, give a suggestion or share an article with the world. To keep messages short, businesses can use shortened URLs by subscribing to providers such as Google URL Shortener, Bitly or TinyURL to ensure that character limits of microblogging platforms are maintained.

2. **Frequent updates:** In order for microblogging to enhance brand awareness, businesses should post messages regularly. Depending on your industry we might recommend one to three posts a day or a week that use different content or are reaching different audiences. Using Search Engine Optimization techniques for microblog posts will expand a business's reach to more potential customers.

3. **Choose the right image:** Many social media platforms support or are entirely driven by images, GIFs and videos. Simply using a photo to deliver a message can be an extremely effective strategy. As the infamous adage says, a picture is worth a thousand words.

4. **Participate and partner.** Social media is meant to be just that: *social*. Positively engaging with followers and other businesses will help build a brand's reputation. Businesses can share another company's post or tag a follower to reply to their message. These are great ways to boost your following, increase your revenue and contribute to your local community.

Microblogging is a great way to improve Search Engine Optimization, engage with potential and existing customers, enhance brand awareness and support local business.

Microblogging Checklist

- ❑ Does the business have a Twitter account?
- ❑ Is the business information provided on the account homepage?
- ❑ Does the business prompt others to comment on the newsfeed?
- ❑ How many followers does the business have?
- ❑ How many accounts is the business following themselves?
- ❑ Is the account regularly updated?
- ❑ Do the updates invite new customers to events?
- ❑ Is the page customized?
- ❑ Do the different social media accounts link to Twitter?
- ❑ Does the business have a Tumblr account?

What's Your Score?

Rate your business based upon the answers to the previous questions.

How Many You Have		Score
0	=	0
1-3	=	30
4-6	=	60
7-9	=	80
10+	=	90

Your Microblogging Score = _____

Suggestions, Tips & Tools

Now that you have an understanding of what microblogging is we can examine the techniques and strategies used for the most commonly used micro-blog platforms.

Leading social networking websites such as Facebook, Twitter, LinkedIn and Google+, also have their own microblogging feature, better known as "status updates".

Twitter for Business

Twitter is a short message communication tool that allows you to send out messages (tweets) up to 140 characters long to people who subscribe to you (followers). Your tweets can include a link to any web content (blog post, website page, PDF document, etc.) or a photograph or video. If a picture is worth a thousand words, adding an image to a tweet greatly expands what you can share to beyond the 140-character limit for tweets. People follow (subscribe) to your Twitter account and you follow other people. This allows you to read, reply to and easily share tweets with your followers (retweet).

Twitter is unique from other platforms because in the social media world, it falls into the category of micro-blogging tools due to the short, disconnected messages it distributes. Twitter shares some features with the most common social media tools (Facebook, Pinterest, LinkedIn, Google+ and YouTube). However, the differences are what defines Twitter.

- Facebook: A tweet is like a short Facebook status update. However, with Twitter, every tweet displays in every follower's feed, apart from nonaffiliated mentions and replies

- Pinterest: Both allow you to share photographs and provide commentary in your post. However, with Twitter, it's much easier to have conversation around a shared image than with the comment feature on Pinterest.

- LinkedIn: A tweet is like a short LinkedIn status update. While LinkedIn is based on trust relationships (and two-way agreements), Twitter allows you to follow anyone, including strangers. This is helpful when you target potential customers.

- Google+: A tweet is like a short Google+ status update. Twitter also allows you to organize people into lists that organize conversations similar to Google+ groups.

- YouTube: A tweet can contain a link to a video. However, Twitter doesn't allow you to create a video channel or organize your videos for easy location and commentary.

For a successful social media footprint, writing the perfect tweet is like an art that can lead to, really, any possibility. Besides more exposure for your business, you may find yourself a viral hit and a popular Tweeter worldwide. Here are some sure fire ways to increase the popularity of your tweets:

- **Tweet at (@) already popular accounts:** You want to remain connected with influencers, especially those who might be inclined to use your product, support it and give it positive PR. These influencers are included, but not limited to, celebrities, pseudo-celebrities and local-celebrities, popular bloggers and popular Twitter accounts in your area. Do this by mentioning them in a tweet or even direct messaging them. Be careful not to spam anyone because that may turn some people away from your product.

- **Use hashtags (#):** Make use of trending hashtags to increase followers and retweets. If you use a hashtag that is trending, it will drive up traffic and your tweets will appear whenever anyone clicks on the trending hashtag. This may help make your account become popular. Better yet, use something that is trending nationally, or something pretty generic, along the lines of #mondaymotivation, with a relevant tweet on Monday of course, or the ever popular #treatyoself.

- **Be funny:** Do not be afraid to use humor. If you have something funny or clever to say about a relevant or trending event, then tweet it (provided it isn't overtly offensive or vulgar). Who knows, it might become a viral hit.

- **Spark interest through images:** Tweet images of your product or service, as well as links to your website to drive up traffic and grow interest. Make sure your Instagram, Facebook and Twitter are all linked together. After all, you cannot expect others to connect to you if you are not connected to yourself via all outlets.

While becoming popular on twitter is easier said than done, these strategies are a great way to drive traffic and draw in customers for your business. Now that you know how to create a more popular Twitter account, let us dive into how you can use Twitter for your business. Twitter is a microblogging site with 313 million monthly active users (second quarter of 2016).[9] With these statistics in mind, it is no wonder why businesses choose to engage in this key aspect of social media. Here are five top ways you can use Twitter to help grow your business:

1. **Network with people:** Find people with similar interests or who have an interest in your business by joining industry and topic groups related to your business. This can be done via sites like www.twibes.com and could help you find new clients, new partners and get referrals.

2. **Monitor Your Brand and Reputation through Twitter Search:** You can see what people are saying about your brand. This feature helps you revise your strategies and ultimately grow your business.

3. **Conduct Market Research:** By following experts, companies, competitors and leaders in your industry, you will be able to conduct informal market research. This will help you build expertise in your industry and consequently build your credibility.

4. **Promote and Broadcast Content:** Informing your audience about upcoming events, promotions, new products, important news, etc. is very valuable. You can also have your Tweets reposted on other social media websites, such as Facebook and LinkedIn. Consistently sharing valuable information helps your business gain exposure and increase brand awareness.

---

9 *See the Reference section at the end of the book for further information and sources*

5. **Provide Customer Service:** By sharing tips, helping others with problems or questions and linking to helpful articles posted elsewhere, you are able to provide customer service through Twitter. Active communication on Twitter cannot only help you get new customers, but also build strong relationships with current customers.

Following these five simple steps can go a long way in marketing and developing your business.

CHAPTER 12
KEY 6
RICH MEDIA

"To swear off making mistakes is very easy. All you have to do is swear off having ideas."
— Leo Burnett, Founder, Leo Burnett Worldwide

RICH MEDIA IS eye catching and is useful for attracting new customers and entertaining audiences. Rich media is stimulating to the senses and sticks in the minds of potential and current customers. People tend to take you and your business more seriously if the quality of your website images and media are great. This is also an area in which you can get creative – strive to put forward a product that viewers will want to share with others. The more captivating your media, the more views you will get and the more likely it will be remembered. Stephen Mitroff (2015) explains in *Perception and Human Processing*, "Visual search is the process of finding specific target items within an environment using particular visual feature or prior knowledge." He goes on to explain, "Visual searches take place in everyday, innocuous contexts such as finding your car in a parking lot, and in critical contexts, such as finding enemy combatants in an urban battlefield." Rich media adds to your brand recognition. Wherever you look and in whatever form, if you add rich media you engage, motivate, and convert better. Add a video to your homepage, images to Facebook, 6-second videos to Twitter, etc. It can be found in blogging, websites, or microblogging, social networks, or even review sites.

Rich media refers to the utilization of various technologies to enhance a recipient's experience. The term rich media is not easy to define. All rich media technologies generally exhibit at least some of the following characteristics:

- Allows for advanced animations
- Support audio/radio in advertisements
- Make it possible for instant user interactions

The defining characteristic of rich media is that the media element exhibits dynamic motion. This motion can occur over time or in response to an interaction with the user.

Examples of Rich Media

YouTube, iTunes, SoundCloud, Podcasts, Spotify, Flickr, Snapchat, Instagram, Vine, Vimeo, Pinterest

Benefits of Using Rich Media

Rich media can be a very powerful online advertising tool. The following are reasons why using rich media can be a successful marketing tool:

- Appeals to the senses – The eye is drawn to visual sources, like an image or video.

- Attracts new customers – If the quality of your website or media is great, people will assume the quality of your business is also great.

- Entertains your audience – Get creative with images and videos to satisfy your customers. Strive to put forward a product viewers will want to share.

- High interaction rate - Rich media has functions like video and movement. Customers may be able to engage with the rich media. This interaction may improve brand awareness and message association.

Key Learning - Focus on developing a well-constructed website with high quality images and interesting video content. People are drawn to this and it will also give you a more professional appearance. Videos also improve your Search Engine Optimization (SEO), because the more videos and slideshows you have, the higher they will appear when people search for you, your company, or related terms.

Puppy Dogs, Ice Cream and Money

When it comes to images, my philosophy is puppy dogs, ice cream and money. The puppy is cute and enticing. The ice cream is a tasty craving. The money is desire and flash. What you need to do for your business is figure out what the "puppy dog" is, what the "ice cream" is, and what the "money" is. Then take pictures of these things, come up with a collection and rotate them in your postings.

For example, if you have a retail store, you have clothing, jewelry and people wearing these things. "Puppies" would be a really attractive material or outfit. "Ice cream" would be a good-looking person wearing that outfit. "Money" is an outfit with the logo, showing the prestige. For *each* business there are puppy dogs, ice cream and money.

Best Practices for Creating Rich Media

The term rich media may sound new, but it is exactly the opposite. The reason for labeling this sort of media as rich is because of its advanced technological features. No matter where we are, we encounter rich media every day and are able to involve and interact with these advertisements. Transforming your ads into rich media may seem like a difficult task, so I have compiled several ways that you can successfully create your own rich media:

1. **Diversity**: Using a variety of advanced technological features in rich media can add more fullness. Different features added into your rich media can add more fun, engagement and interaction with your viewers.

2. **Relevance:** It is important to employ features to your rich media that bring out the best in your product.

3. **Consistency:** Consistency does not refer to the frequency of putting out rich media. It actually means the consistency of the rich media with your brand image.

4. **Creativity:** Bring something new to the table. Make your rich media as eye catching and unique as possible to leave a strong impression.

If you find it difficult to remember these tips, simply remind yourself of my puppy dogs, ice cream and money philosophy and you will be on the right track.

Creating a High-Quality Video

If you are looking to build rapport with new and existing customers, begin thinking about creating a video for your website. If you are not sure how to go about it, below are 5 tips and tricks for planning and making a video:

1. **Know What Your Goal Is**: Be clear on what the take away message will be from your video. Do you want viewers to see your product in use, understand your range of services, or be educated in a topic area? Each of these goals requires a separate technique in order to be effective. For example, educating your audience will require you to rehearse your content, hone in on the key message quickly and restate it at least once. On the other hand, demonstrating a product will likely require more advanced filming and videography planning with less spoken word.

2. **Short and Sweet:** Videos are best when short and deliver only one or two take away messages. Keeping your videos to 2 minutes or less will ensure that the viewer listens to your message and will keep their attention until the end.

3. **Quality Sound:** It is important for your video's sound to be clear without background noise. With advances in technology most laptops are equipped with high quality sound recording tools. Make sure any recordings are done in a quiet area, but be careful not to use an empty room. Furnished rooms, particularly rooms with carpet, will help absorb background noise to provide clear sound for your video.

4. **Crisp Visuals:** If you cannot afford to outsource your video production to a professional company, all hope is not lost. There are several free options you can use such as Windows Movie Maker and iMovie for PCs and Macs. Whether you outsource this or do it yourself, pay close attention to the visuals used. If the video is of a speaker, make sure that the background is not distracting and the speaker is easy to follow. Movement in the video should be smooth and controlled and the video should be recorded in a well-lit area.

Using Videos for Search Engine Optimization and Conversion Rate Optimization

Making a high quality video can improve your brand's reputation, build a connection and develop familiarity with you and your customers. Creating a high quality video can also improve your Search Engine Optimization (SEO) and Conversion Rate Optimization (CRO).

Rich media, especially videos on your website, are huge for Search Engine Optimization (SEO) and Conversion Rate Optimization (CRO). The reason why videos are very powerful for Search Engine Optimization is because the text of the video is transcribed by Google, so if you say certain words or phrases in the video, your video and therefore, your website, ends up ranking higher in searches.

Additionally, part of how Google and other search engines rank sites is by the amount of time people spend on the sites they go to. The longer people stay on your site, the higher ranking you will receive. When people watch videos that you post on your website, they stay longer on your website. This increases the power of your website.

Conversion Rate Optimization is how many people come to your website and take some sort of action (convert). Videos make it much easier for people to understand who you are and what you do. This understanding will cause more people to engage with you and your business and take action (unless the product is awful).

Rich Media Checklist

- ❏ In a basic Google search of the business are there any video results?
- ❏ Any image results?
- ❏ Does the business website contain any videos?
- ❏ Any images that appear in a slideshow?
- ❏ Does the business have a YouTube channel?
- ❏ Does the business have a Flickr account?
- ❏ If the accounts exist are there sufficient links from the website?
- ❏ Are those accounts customized?
- ❏ Are there any iTunes results for the business podcast?

What's Your Score?

Rate your business based upon the answers to the previous questions.

How Many You Have		Score
0	=	0
1-3	=	30
4-6	=	60
7-9	=	80
10+	=	90

Your Rich Media Score = _____

Suggestions, Tips & Tools

Understanding how to use rich media in your business is important for growth. Below are ways that you can use current rich media platforms to enhance your business.

YouTube for Business

With over a billion users, YouTube is a platform that every business owner needs to consider as part of their marketing strategy. Every day people watch hundreds of millions of hours on YouTube that generates billions of views.[10] After all, most potential customers would much rather watch an informative video of your company's products and services than read a lengthy sales letter.

Not only is YouTube a great promotional tool, but you can also use the video host to create trust, authority and recognition by creating a channel for your business. Here are a few ways to do so:

1. **Showcase Your Products/Services:** Many successful businesses use video marketing as their primary strategy to introduce customers to their products and services. From explainer videos, to webinars, to video presentations and more, there are many different ways to showcase what your company offers to your target market.

---

10 *See the Reference section at the end of the book for further information and sources*

A great example of a company that uses YouTube to market their products is GoPro, one of the most popular camera choices in the world today. The company has used the channel to upload content ranging from informational videos on new products to compilations of footage from customers using their cameras.

2. **Demonstrate Your Expertise:** YouTube is the second largest search engine on the Internet today, behind its parent company, Google. Every day, users search for answers to their questions and problems. This presents a great opportunity to build authority for your business, and reach your target audience by offering expertise in the form of short videos with advice and tips.

   For example, an internet marketing firm could create short videos filled with tips on, "How to Utilize SEO" or "5 Great Social Media Marketing Strategies". By creating short videos, 3-5 minutes, with great tips, you are demonstrating expertise for your industry and are building more awareness for your business.

3. **Give a Behind the Scenes Look:** Why not give your current and potential customers a behind-the-scenes look at how your business runs its operations? Not only is this an effective way to build trust with those interested in the business, but it is also a great way to show how hard your company works for its customers. You could feature an interview with the CEO, introduce your staff, or even vlog (video blog) a day at work.

4. **Customer Testimonials:** Another way to build trust and awareness for a business is by uploading videos of customer testimonials to YouTube. Showcasing positive recommendations and reviews from past customers is a proven factor for success. Testimonials make purchase decisions easier and help ensure people that they are being served by a company with a positive track record.

5. **Creating Video Tutorials to Help Customers:** Watching a video tutorial with instructions on how to set up or use a product is much more helpful than trying to understand a complicated user manual. Can your business make things easier with video tutorials? If so, YouTube is a great platform to provide customers

with instructions as they can always forward, pause or reverse your video tutorials to follow instructions at their own pace.

Another fantastic benefit of uploading video tutorials is that you can offer support and assistance in the YouTube comments. If users have any questions or difficulties, then they can leave a comment under the video on YouTube. Make sure to have notifications enabled, so you can respond with assistance and support.

In addition to these five ways to use YouTube for your business, there are many helpful ways to use the popular platform as an essential part of your marketing plan. Depending on the nature of your business, hosting live streams, creating Q&A videos, providing conference/event recaps, featuring expert interviews, making company announcements and much more are very useful techniques in integrating YouTube into your marketing plan.

Not only does YouTube allow a business to gain more exposure through video marketing, but the platform also helps connect businesses with current and potential customers through video comments. There is no better time to utilize YouTube as a marketing tool to build more authority, trust and market reach, than right now.

Podcasts for Business

Combine the words "broadcast" and "iPod" to enter into the world of Podcasts. Podcasts are a very popular form of media in today's marketplace. Podcasts are radio-style talk shows that are not live. It is like having the Internet and the Radio on demand. These are pre-recorded by individuals and businesses so that they are available to be purchased and downloaded by listeners at their own disposal. Podcasts have exploded in attractiveness because they take very little time to make, are very low cost, can reach a widespread audience and can be listened to at your own convenience. All you *really* need to create a good podcast is a computer, a mic and the Internet. Although you do not need much to create a podcast, there are ways that you can amplify your content so that your listeners stay intrigued. Here are some best practices to follow when entering into the dynamic world of recording podcasts:

- **Plan:** Nothing is worse than being unprepared. Go into a podcast session with an idea and strategy of what you are going to talk about. If you do not, it will waste valuable time and require a lot of editing.

- **Edit:** Get inexpensive or free editing software because you will make mistakes. It is human nature. Make sure everything you record is actually worth listening to and you are not rambling on or off track. Also, be mindful of the noise levels. Try to keep the sound level as consistent as possible. Get rid of any excess noise because it makes it easier for your audience to listen.

- **Have Guests:** As interesting as you probably are, it is nice to have a different perspective on the topics or themes you discuss. Bring in fascinating guests to interview that have exciting experiences to talk about.

- **Unique Content:** Be sure that the topics you are talking about are actually of interest to your audience. Otherwise, you will be left without listeners. Keep your audience engaged by having interesting topics, well-known guests speak on your podcast, etc. Think outside the box and be original.

- **Pick a Name:** Think of something that your audience will remember. After all, this is what you will be known by and is what will show up in Google searches.

- **Be Relaxed:** Nothing is worse than being able to notice when a person speaking is nervous. It makes everyone else feel uncomfortable. Relax and enjoy yourself. Just remember this: if you make a mistake, you can always edit it.

Through podcasts your business will be able to tell a story. The purpose of podcasts is to educate, entertain, inspire, encourage and stimulate emotions in your listeners. However, the single most important function of podcasts is the ability to connect the creators with listeners. People are able to develop a bond through podcasts.

Snapchat for Business

Who knew Snapchat, a mobile app released in 2011, would have such a powerful business influence today? Snapchat is one of the most effective applications used to connect people. Its main feature is temporary content and it keeps all of us on our toes as we use the app constantly to stay informed. Here are ways to use Snapchat as a business tool:

1. **Targeting Younger Audiences:** It is without a doubt that a majority of users of Snapchat are people under the age of 30. If your business needs to appeal to teenagers or young adults, using a Snapchat account is a great way to showcase that your company or business is in touch with the latest social media platform.

2. **Constant Brand Awareness:** People check their phones more than they shop or browse the web, so it is important for a business to use that to its advantage. Snapchat allows users to send photos or short videos to each other. Users can also post their snaps to their collective Snapstory, which shows up on their followers' news feed. Businesses can give their customers or consumers a special perspective through their Snapstory, as well as keep a visual presence on people's news feed. Your business can also use brand ambassadors that have a large reach that use your product/service to promote the business if you do not have a large following on your own account.

3. **Temporary Promotional Deals:** People routinely check Snapchat because the content has a 24-hour lifespan. Use this brevity to your advantage, because people do not want to miss out on announcements or special promotions. If a business snaps a discount code or important announcements, customers will be more inclined to both check your Snapstory and spend their money. The business utilizes free marketing and the customers get a discount – it is a win-win.

Give Snapchat a try and see your business competitively grow while staying up to date with this latest social media platform. *Start snapping today!*

Instagram for Business

Upload, Edit, Share – It is as simple as that. Instagram offers a unique, inexpensive and easy way to market a business and create a community with customers. If you are launching a startup business, Instagram is a great way for you to create rapid buzz and growth for your company on a medium with over 500 million monthly active users (as of June 2016).[11]

Instagram is a social networking site entirely based on photos and videos. You can follow other people, comment on photos and discover new users and businesses through hashtags – a simple and effective way of marking your posts by its subject material.

Here are 7 tips to maximize your Instagram account:

1. **Keep It Simple:** When creating an Instagram account, try to use a simple username so customers can find you easily. Introduce your business and services briefly in the bio section and add a profile picture that most users will be able to easily recognize as your company.

2. **Appealing Content:** One of the appeals of Instagram to many of its users is its clean and simple design. This allows for more focus on the content of each post. Creating beautiful and captivating pictures is key to making your business's image more attractive. With Instagram's preprogrammed filters and editing tools, you can add a professional touch to enhance your images taken right off your phone. However, be careful not to make your images appear overly edited.

3. **Personalization:** Add a personal aspect to your photos by sharing behind the scenes experiences or images of a lifestyle made possible through the assistance of your business. For example, GoPro gives

---

11 *See the Reference section at the end of the book for further information and sources*

a taste of what stunning experiences can be captured with their extreme action and all-purpose durable camera.

4. **Connect to Other Social Media Accounts:** Once you have covered the content you wish to produce, it is time to cultivate a following and build a community. To increase your follower count, start by connecting your Instagram account to any other social media you use, including Facebook and Twitter. You can also embed a link to your profile on your company's website. Make sure to start following those who follow you and other users to help expand your network.

5. **Interact with Users:** Commenting and liking posts boosts your user-friendly nature and online presence. You can reply to a comment or directly mention a specific user by using the @ sign before their username (ex. @Netflix). Becoming familiar with your customers opens the door to constructive feedback. Asking your followers to share their opinion on a product or experience with a service can improve the quality of your business by adjusting to your customers' needs and wants.

6. **Use #Hashtags:** Hashtags are an easy and effective way to label and market each photo with associated phrases or adjectives. For example, if you are promoting your San Francisco restaurant's fresh strawberry lemonade, you could add hashtags such as #SanFrancisco, #SF, #StrawberryLemonade, #Summer, or #Refreshing. If a user searches for any of those keywords in the Discover portion of Instagram, your post would automatically appear. However, try to keep your number of hashtags small and effective.

7. **Capitalize on Trends:** Using trending or popular hashtags are great integrative marketing strategies to widen your online market. Posting a photo to accompany #MothersDay, #SpringBreak, or #BlackFriday will market your service or product to customers looking for ideas, presents, or good deals.

Now that you understand the basics of the Instagram interface, you can start to use some of these efficient and integrative marketing services to promote and expand your business by:

- **Displaying New Services or Products:** Instagram is a quick and useful way to inform your customers of new offers from your business. Whether your business is introducing a new summer line of fashion or now serving Happy Hour, your followers will be the first to know. Starbucks keeps its customers coming in by announcing new drinks and treats available via their Instagram page.

- **Offering Exclusive Deals:** Maintain your audience by giving your followers a special incentive through exciting specials. This marketing strategy will help bring in more customer interest and revenue. One way to do this is simply by advertising special offers coming up in the near future, such as Ben and Jerry's #FreeConeDay. Another way is to provide instructions in your post on how to receive an exclusive deal, such as using a coupon code or displaying proof at the register that they follow your business online.

- **Promoting Through Others:** Create a business specific hashtag that will allow your customers to use it whenever they post a photo of or use your product or service. For example, if you own a dining establishment, you can advertise your hashtag on the menu and ask for your customers to use it if they choose to post a photo. Then, their followers will know where to go to get the same product. Taco Bell's popular expression, #FourthMeal, can be used by anyone posting a photo enjoying a Taco Bell meal.

Hopefully this will help you get started using Instagram as a strategic and innovative marketing technique. The possibilities are endless so be creative and have fun.

Pinterest for Business

Pinterest is an interactive, pinboard formatted website that allows users to showcase collections of different things they are interested in. Whether it is food, clothing, or different locations, Pinterest is a free service for users to visually bookmark these images ("pins") into different collections of images ("pin boards").

Evan Sharp, one of the co-founders of Pinterest, describes the pinning process as something that increases the chances of a user running into the same image, or other media, multiple times. Once a user pins something onto a board, the name of that board becomes the string that describes that pin. Another user may pin the same thing onto their own board, which could be named something else—such as 'streetwear attire,' 'birthday gifts' or 'wedding designs.' Sharp says that this creates "thousands of human-generated strings" that describe each image and creates a way for people to help solve each other's search problems.

Growing in popularity with other social media platforms, such as Facebook, Twitter and Instagram, Pinterest has also become another marketing tool for start-up businesses. Pinterest offers a new way for businesses to communicate and connect with customers. It allows potential customers to handpick different items and brands they like and to follow different pin boards that may relate to a certain business' product or brand.

Pinterest is basically a digital scrapbook where you can "pin" (post) and "like" the images you are interested in and users can follow each other. We outline below how businesses can use Pinterest as a social media platform to promote and share their products. For all types of business, Pinterest is another social media platform to increase their brand awareness and opportunities. Businesses have several techniques available to them in creating search optimization for Pinterest users to find their products easily. Here are some best practices:

1. **Include Keywords:** Within the description of pinned images, be sure to provide keywords such as 'how to' for products that include tutorials for their use.

2. **Use Interesting and High Quality Photos**: Higher quality and creative product photos are the key to getting pinners' attention. You don't see a pixelated and blurry photo that is repined by pinners. Before you pin your product photo, make it fun and interesting to grab attention. Another technique is posting longer images that are appealing to the eye when viewed from a mobile device, as well as from a computer screen. The goal is to make your pins look visually appealing.

3. **Share a Story Instead of Promoting Your Product**: Add an interesting story or description to your product to make pinners re-pin it. Do not make pinners think you just want to sell a product to them.

4. **Study Your Target Audience**: You can use Pinterest as a market research tool to find out what are the products, colors or styles that get the most repins. You can also can study demography, who and what are the ages most likely to repin and like your product.

5. **Review Other Businesses Pin Boards**: You can use it to see how your competitors do on Pinterest. You can see what they are doing well, areas where they can improve and use that in your methods.

6. **Create a Contest**: Everyone likes a free gift. You can leverage Pinterest as a platform to execute advertising by creating a contest. It will tempt a pinner to repin therefore increasing your brand presence.

The most popular topics on Pinterest are related to food and drink, crafts, home decor and women's fashion. Due to these facts, restaurants, crafts stores and women's retail stores in particular will benefit the most by pinning.

Etsy is a business that uses Pinterest's predominantly visual platform to showcase their brand. Etsy is an online marketplace for individuals and businesses to sell their hand-made, vintage or art products and supplies. New pins are posted daily on Etsy's board - taken from items within the Etsy marketplace, content inspired by other trending Pinterest boards and from weekly 'Guest Pinners' invited to bring in new content from their own finds. Etsy also integrated a 'Pin It' button onto etsy.com for shoppers to easily pin items while browsing their site.

Stitch Fix is another business that uses Pinterest. It utilizes more of Pinterest's categorizing visual scheme into their online service. Stitch Fix is a personal styling service that allows clients to provide personal Pinterest links and pin boards onto their profile. This gives stylists a sense of what items customers like and would want to purchase.

CHAPTER 13
KEY 7
MOBILE MARKETING

"It is not the strongest species that survive, nor the most intelligent, but the most responsive to change."

— Charles Darwin, Naturalist

10 YEARS AGO I said, "Mobile is the future." Today that future has arrived. We see it around us, younger generation to older generation, everyone is on their phones. What was an interesting development in 2008 has become in many ways, the Internet for many people. It is not just marketing to mobile, but marketing WITH your mobile device.

Mobile devices are unlocking opportunities for marketers on a new scale. It has the potential to be a tremendous enabler. Have your company focus on getting the basics of a mobile marketing strategy right. These include:

- Ensure your website is mobile-friendly

- Start communicating with customers through SMS marketing campaigns

- Build on your search engine marketing campaign for mobile

- Invest in mobile advertising

In today's society, people are always on their smartphones. Mobile marketing and mobile apps are not just for big brands or companies. More and more small and midsize businesses are following the mobile trend and understanding that an effective mobile strategy involves more than just a mobile-friendly website.

Examples of Mobile Marketing

Mobile Apps, SMS Text, Foursquare

Benefits of Using Mobile Marketing

Interact in real-time with your customers as they search and find, read reviews at the point of contact and proceed to purchase. The average person spends 90 minutes a day on their phone, which amounts to 23 days a year and 3.9 years of an average person's life spent staring at their phone screen. 80% of mobile device time is spent on apps.[12] If those statistics are not enough to convince you of the importance of developing a mobile marketing strategy, the following are benefits you can incur from doing so:

- Maintain contact and visibility – People look at their mobile screens more than ever, which makes it an easy avenue to connect.

- Mobile is arguably the closest you can get to a consumer - There is no other device that is as personal. Mobile devices are with you all the time and everyone has one.

Key Learning - Focus on making your business as accessible as possible for people to find by making your website mobile friendly with at least a responsive design and having your own company dedicated mobile application at the higher level.

---

12 *See the Reference section at the end of the book for further information and sources*

Developing a Mobile App

At the very least, a mobile ready website is critical, no matter what your business. To be on the Internet today is to be mobile. Here are the top 5 reasons to consider makinga business mobile app for your business:

1. **Be Visible to Customers at All Times:** While probably only a handful of applications make up the bulk of the total mobile usage, it does not change the fact that each user has to unlock, scroll and scan their device for the apps they are looking for. Being "in the way" can be an advantage to your company, as our mind unconsciously does record every image and text (or well-designed app icon) it comes across — even if it happens unnoticed.

2. **Create a Direct Marketing Channel:** Apps serve many functions: they can provide general info, prices, booking forms, search features, user accounts, messengers, news feeds and much more. One of the biggest benefits of having a mobile app is that all the information you would like to provide to your customers – including special sales and promotions – is right at their fingertips. Through push notifications you are getting even closer to a direct interaction and can easily remind customers about your products and services whenever it makes sense to do so.

3. **Build Brand Recognition and Provide Value:** A mobile app for business can greatly contribute to brand awareness. There are two aspects that will make an app a true winner:

    a. Brand: A mobile app is like a blank billboard sign. It is very versatile when it comes to design, whether it's stylish, hip, functional, shocking, or informative. The most important aspect is to create an app that has features customers will love; while simultaneously it is well branded and beautifully designed.

    b. Recognition: The more often customers get involved with the app, the sooner they will be inclined to buy the product and/ or service. In advertising this is called the "effective frequency".

As a rule of thumb, hearing and/or seeing the brand approximately 20 times is what will get the brand truly noticed.

Digitalize the royalty program you have in place, make it possible for your customers to collect their rewards via your mobile app. The result will be more downloads and more return customers.

4. **Improve Customer Engagement:** Customers need a way to reach a business or company. Having a messaging (or help desk) feature within the app can really make a difference in the communication with customers and clients. OpenTable, for example, built its entire business model around this principle. Instead of calling a restaurant for a table, one can be booked with less than five clicks on their platform.

5. **Cultivate Customer Loyalty**: Last, but not least, the most important reason why considering a mobile app is customer loyalty. With all the noise out there — roadside banners, billboards, flashing signs, newspaper ads, flyers, coupons, websites, website banners, Facebook ads, and email marketing — businesses slowly lose impact on customers because of the immense amount of advertising surrounding everything and everyone. It is time to go back to making a true and sincere connection with customers, and making them a loyal customer to a product and/or service.

Mobile Marketing Checklist

- ❑ Has the business created an app specifically for their customers?
- ❑ Does the business show up in a search on mobile app Yelp?
- ❑ Do 'nearby' searches within the mobile Yelp app show the business?
- ❑ Does the business show up in a search for the product/service on Google Maps?
- ❑ Is the business website mobile friendly (responsive design)?

- ❏ Does the mobile website provide proper business/contact information easily?
- ❏ Do these apps offer any medium in which customers can provide feedback?
- ❏ Have a specific iPhone app? Android app?
- ❏ Have a text messaging program?
- ❏ Participate in a mobile customer loyalty program?
- ❏ Does the business use geo tools to target customers walking by the business?

What's Your Score?

Rate your business based upon the answers to the previous questions.

How Many You Have		Score
0	=	0
1-3	=	30
4-6	=	60
7-9	=	80
10+	=	90

Your Mobile Marketing Score = _____

Suggestions, Tips & Tools

The next step for your company, besides making sure your existing website is mobile-friendly and has a responsive design, is to consider creating a mobile application. Mobile applications allow you to have a custom mobile app for your business to communicate messages to your audience. Depending on how much emphasis you would like to put on your mobile strategy, there are two options for developing your mobile app:

1. **Hire an app development agency:** There are services out there that allow you to simply and easily create your mobile application. These services will then add it to the Apple and Google online app stores for people to download to their phones. You can use one of the mobile app builders such as Como, BuildFire, or AppsBuilder to build your own mobile app without having to worry about coding and technicalities.

2. **Bring your own in-house app development team on board:** The next level up is to make a fully customizable app for your business. Typically larger organizations do this. Some of the better custom mobile applications are Starbucks, Domino's Pizza, Uber and many more.

Either way you decide to go, a mobile is going to be a standard component of any business in the future. The choice you make today is going set the foundation for the future of your business tomorrow.

CHAPTER 14
KEY 8
INDUSTRY SPECIFIC

"Acquaintances, in sort, represent a source of social power, and the more acquaintances you have the more powerful you are."

- Malcolm Gladwell, Journalist, Author, Speaker

THE POWER OF third party validation, beyond review sites is that they can drive awareness, fuel your reputation, and in short give fuel to all your other efforts. Depending on what type of business you have, there are industry specific websites, magazines and newspapers that cater to a variety of business categories. Papers are useful local tools to promote your business and connect with similar local businesses. Networking within your specific industry will also keep you up to date on the latest events and developments. Even if networking seems tedious, affiliating yourself with like-minded businesspeople and surrounding yourself with people that you want to aspire to is necessary. Connect in person and on social media with like-minded businesses. Help those who help you, it is always good to return the favor.

Examples of Industry Specific Websites, Magazines and Newspapers

Lawyers.com, Expedia, Vitals.com, Healthgrades.com, Diablo Magazine, Oakland Magazine, San Francisco Chronicle, Business Times Journals.

Benefits of Industry Specific Websites, Magazines and Newspapers

Participate and actively seek opportunities to be featured in publications and media explicitly tailored to your industry. The benefits encompass the ability to:

- Network within your industry – Stay informed on what's the latest and greatest.

- Surround yourself with what you want to become – Affiliate with like-minded businesses.

- Help those who help you – You never know when you'll need a favor,

Key Learning - Focus on growing your business identity online and to find industry specific websites and networking groups to promote your business. Creating content that is worth looking at and developing relationships with a list of writers in your area is very helpful for getting featured in media publications.

Importance of Being Featured in Media

Starting and keeping a business is tougher than ever before. Businesses have to get the attention of their target audience and get them to check out their product or service, while simultaneously taking into consideration the competitors in the industry. Most startups want to get their business featured on every form of press release possible such as blogs, newspapers, magazines, TV, or radio. What is the importance in doing so?

Companies, big or small, want to promote their product or service through intermediaries. Why? Most people act based on their perception of facts. Getting featured boosts an organization's credibility and brand recognition. It is a way of getting the company's image and message to its customers, investors, possible business partners and the general public. Another advantage of this is that press highlights the business in all aspects, not just focusing on the product or service the company offers. Eventually, successful advertising through media can lead to the achievement of the company's objectives.

How Do You Get Major Press for Your Business?

Every industry has their own associations, magazines, websites, newspapers and other publications. This is where you want to look for ways to connect. Here are helpful tips to get featured on different forms of press:

1. **Create content that's really worth endorsing:** Pitch a story, not just a product/service. The main purpose of doing the pitch is to promote your business. Tying the business to a trending current event will make your pitch more relevant. Discover the value proposition of what your company does and how it solves a problem people are encountering. Collect and create data that has never been in the media before. This will draw attention from the press.

2. **Construct a targeted list of writers and journalists:** Identify the best writers in your area who will be most likely to benefit from your pitch or story. Make sure your story aligns with their experience and area of focus. This will increase the possibilities of your pitch being published or featured because writers are always on the hunt for good and relevant content.

3. **Let the journalists know you have read/watched their work:** Most people reply best when they are shown attention or when they are given a compliment regarding their recent article or achievement. Showing personal interest to your target list of writers will show

that you are thoughtful and respectful, therefore, worth their time and effort.

4. **Give them a shout out**

When you have successfully pitched your story and are featured on your targeted press, return the favor by acknowledging them on your site. Allocate a page on your site to save these references. Do not forget to share stories on your social media to let the public know how they have made an impact on your company.

These tips mean nothing if you do not put in the effort to promote your business. Rejections from media are inevitable but you must keep trying. Attending professional networking events and workshops could help you increase the chances of connecting with a number of great writers and journalists.

Listing Your Business on Websites

List your business on as many sites as possible. No matter what industry you are in, this will increase your Search Engine Optimization (SEO) because these sites will link back to your business. For example, if you are a physician there are over 60 sites that are dedicated to healthcare, doctors and other related fields. By listing your business on sites that are specific to your industry, you will rank higher when it comes to a search of these things. If you do not know which sites to list your business on, one of the easiest ways to find them is to do a search of your industry or product on Google or other search engines. Instead of looking at the first or second page, go to the ninth or tenth pages of the search. These will typically be the industry specific sites you are looking for. They are not as popular, but they are very specific to your industry.

Be an Award Winner!

Another way to build your presence through industry specific marketing is through award sites. Every industry, area, geography and product/service has awards (local magazines have awards, local community service groups have awards, national publications have awards, etc.). What you want to do is nominate your business for these awards. These awards will ask for information about your business including your website information, address, phone number, paragraph about you, products/services you offer and more. Not only does this create exposure for your brand, but again this increases Search Engine Optimization (SEO) which improves the chances you will be recognized in your industry.

Industry Specific Checklist

- ❑ Has the business been featured in any local media?
- ❑ Any national media?
- ❑ Listed on local sites in your area?
- ❑ Belong to any industry specific group(s) for type of business?
- ❑ Did the group provide reviews/feedback about the particular business?
- ❑ Does the group provide networking for the business?
- ❑ Does the group promote consumer interaction?
- ❑ Are there any conventions that the business attends? Or conferences the company is part of?
- ❑ Has the business hosted or promoted industry specific events?
- ❑ Have any articles been written about the business on industry specific websites?
- ❑ Has the business been featured on a television segment? Radio?
- ❑ Has the business won any awards? (E.g. Super Lawyer, Best of..)
- ❑ Any awards or industry specific affiliations listed on company website?

What's Your Score?

Rate your business based upon the answers to the previous questions.

How Many You Have		Score
0	=	0
1-3	=	30
4-6	=	60
7-9	=	80
10+	=	90

Your Industry Specific Score = _____

Suggestions, Tips & Tools

It is important that you tailor your networking, reach and connections toward your specific industry and target consumer.

HARO for Business

Getting your personal brand out there for the world to see and connect with can be very difficult. Press and media for your business can be heightened by HARO, short for Help A Reporter Out. This service allows journalists to get information from many sources around the world for their upcoming stories. It also provides opportunities for these sources to secure valuable media coverage from helping the reporter out with their story. Journalists seek expert advice, tips, tools, suggestions and more on different subjects from professionals in different industries. HARO works on a mutual trust between its sources and the journalist. HARO is a great resource to use and one you should absolute be using if you are concerned with getting your personal or professional brand out there, building connects with important influences, bloggers and journalists.

HARO is used by many major media outlets and can lead to invaluable publicity for your company. These media outlets include Reuters, Fox News, Chicago Tribune, TIME, Mashable, Refinery29, The New York Times, The Globe and Mail, WSJ, ABC and many more. How do you register to become a source? It's pretty simple. Follow these easy three easy steps:

1. **Sign Up**: Register for free to join HARO through their website (www.helpareporter.com). You will then be connected with over 35,000+ journalists looking for sources from expert professionals

2. **Check for New Stories Daily**: HARO sends out source requests Monday-Friday, three times daily. Look for requests to be a source on stories that are relevant to your expertise, experience or industry.

3. **Pitch Yourself**: Just because you have the experience, does not mean the journalist will pick you as their source. Think about this: there are over 475,000 other HARO users who may have similar experience to you. It is your job to sell yourself to the reporter so that they will pick you as their source. To be picked, include your bio explaining what makes you qualified to answer the question, address any specific requirements/qualifications, and make sure you answer *every* question the journalist asked for. If the journalist is interested in what you said, they will reach out to you.

HARO presents a great opportunity to get you and your business featured in national and local media outlets. However, try not to get discouraged if a journalist does not pick you as their source. It can take an immense amount of effort to be featured. You may be answering source requests multiple times before a journalist reaches out to you. Just remember that all it takes is one opportunity to get increased exposure. HARO will open your world and your brand to endless possibilities.

Networking for Business

Network. Network... And network some more. Networking within your industry is critical to any business that wants to grow and expand. Your business should continually be seeking any media or events in your area that will help grow your organization. You can find opportunities by tapping into your network of friends, family members and acquaintances. One great option to network comes from events in your area. To find networking events, you can check out Eventbrite, Meetup, Rotary, Chamber of Commerce, City Websites and other event sites for your area.

Professionals and business owners need to cultivate more contacts or network better in order to create opportunities. What if you could create 50% more opportunities from the contacts you already have? By leveraging the power of the Internet and Social Media, you can leverage and increase the value out of current and new contacts. Your connections represent a source of social power and the more connections you have the more power you have. Leverage social media networks to expand your professional and personal brand to lead to new sales, more marketplace awareness and for career advancement.

Turn Your Networking Endeavors into Gold

Knowing the right people can take you to places you might not otherwise reach. The goal is to cultivate your contacts. Whether that is reaching out to friends you know, family members working in the industry you are interested in or new individuals that you just met at a networking event, start building a wide range of contacts. The more people you know, the easier it gets. If you do not know how to network effectively, or you are shy, there are some practices to follow to better connect with others. Here are some tips on how to better network at events you attend, as a way to generate new business:

- **Set Realistic Expectations:** Have a goal for why you are attending. Pick events or workshops that align with your aspirations and interests. Know what it is that you are looking for beforehand and be realistic about the potential outcomes.

- **Listen and Learn:** A lot of people forget that networking is more than just talking. Instead, it is all about listening. You can learn a lot about someone by simply listening to them. Let the other person speak more than you. This way you will have gotten to know them a lot better.

- **Show Sincerity and Interest:** Be engaged and show the person that you are attentive to what they have to say. Treat people like friends. This builds an atmosphere of trust. People are more likely to do business with those that they trust.

- **Find a Common Ground:** Discover things that you both have in common. It is easier to talk about things that you both can relate to. Look for mutual likes, dislikes, interests, etc. Finding a common ground is a great stepping stone for building a relationship.

- **Ask Thought-Provoking Questions:** Everyone knows the most asked questions, "What's your name?", "Where are you from?", "What do you do?". Yes, it is important to ask those questions, however, stand out from others by asking genuine and thoughtful questions. However, be mindful not to ask silly or inappropriate questions.

- **Be yourself:** Do not pretend to be someone you are not. It is easy to read through people. Relax and be yourself.

After a networking event, be sure to follow up with those people that you connected with. It is important to invest time to build mutually beneficial professional relationships. You never know, a connection you made today could lead to an opportunity tomorrow.

Individuals constantly need inspiration to continue to grow themselves as well as an organization. David Mitroff, Ph.D. runs his own professional networking site, Professional Connector (www. ProfessionalConnector.com), and hosts hundreds of networking events in the San Francisco Bay Area and beyond. If you need further help on how to network and give your organization the tools you need to continue to grow and exceed business goals, do not hesitate to visit www.ProfessionalConnector.com.

CHAPTER 15
KEY 9
EVENT MARKETING

"Make every detail perfect, and limit the number of details to perfect."

— Jack Dorsey, Co-Founder, CEO, Twitter

THERE IS NO substitute for face-to-face meetings. Promoting and marketing events to bring people together can be stressful and overwhelming, especially considering all of the various event-promoting sites there are. There are many places that you can choose to promote upcoming events you may have. On your website, it is always a good idea to feature your calendar as much as possible. Use the Internet to publicize your event and make it easier for your audience to gain information about it. Using the Internet is also convenient because you can make changes to the event, quickly notify people of upcoming events and interact with your audience.

Collaborating with others is a good way to relieve some of the burden of creating an entire event. Increase what the event has to offer and offset some of the workload by inviting others to present, provide something at your event, or help promote the event with you. This will help expand your client base as well as theirs. Here are the top 9 tools to promote events:

- **LinkedIn events**: Millions of members have been increasingly utilizing the tool of LinkedIn to source and sign up to attend local or industry related events. It benefits event organizers, marketers and professionals alike.

- **Facebook events**: Create a Facebook page for your event. Include a brief topic description, information regarding any guest speakers, photos of the venue and/ or important guest attendees, event-related videos, and a prominent "register now" button. By doing this on Facebook, you will also be able to reach out more audiences, who are essentially potential customers.

- **Tweet-based**: Post event links on Twitter informing followers about upcoming events. Come up with catchy hashtags (#) to create buzz as well as engage with your audience.

- **Instagram or Pinterest**: Take photos before, during, and after your event and post them. You may also create an event countdown to raise awareness and engage potential customers. During the event, engage the audiences by encouraging them to take pictures and upload them with hashtags to Instagram or Pinterest.

- **Online registration-ticketing platform**: Utilizing online platforms, like Eventbrite and Meetup, allows for a more accessible event, leading to more attendees.

- **Press release**: Do not ignore traditional media. Send press releases to local journalists who may be interested in covering the event.

- **Team up with a Non-Profit**: Your event will attract new target audiences while helping the community. By doing this, it will show that your business is interested in the success and well-being of the local community.

- **Create calendar invitations**: Utilize your company email list when you're having an event, but do not overwhelm your customers with your invitations. Just simply send a reminder about the events as the date draws close. Keep it short and simple.

- **Online promotion**: This includes social media, blogs, and other social networking platforms that specialize on events such as Meetup, LinkedIn and others.

Throwing an event creates brand awareness, customer loyalty, reminds your audience that you exist and results in lead generation. There are two approaches to event promotion. The first option is where you host an event that you actually want people to attend. You map it out, promote it, get people to attend and follow up with attendees. In this approach, you have to put in a fair amount of work to get people to come to the event.

The other approach gives you almost the same benefits, but without as much work. In this option, you do not actually have to throw an event. You will still list the event on all of your social media sites, website and in your email newsletter. You will still invite people, but you do not have to worry about whether anyone shows up or not. These "fake" events are called Question and Answer (Q & A) events. You select a time of the day where you are already at your office or will be at a coffee shop. Whatever time you decide, let people know when and where you will be to answer any questions they may have about what you do or how your business works. For example, if you are a financial services firm, you can say, "Come by our office at 9am to meet with our financial expert and have any of your questions answered." It's as simple as that. If someone wants to come in at that time to have their questions answered, while you are already at the office, then they can.

Keep in mind that this is not a workshop. You do not provide coffee or bagels (unless your office already has it). In fact, you are not providing anything but an answer to their questions. If someone does show up and has questions, that is great. If no one shows up, that's also okay. The odds are that no one will show up, however, six months from now someone will do a Google search on that particular topic. They will find your event and they will call you. The purpose of these "fake" events is so that you will rank higher on search engines, social networks and more importantly stay on the top of mind of people. You can get all of the benefits of doing an event without all the work. Even if no one comes in, that is okay because it still serves the same purpose. It allows you to engage in more ways than you previously had.

We will now talk further about how to do a real event, however, many of the techniques also work for "fake" events.

Examples of Event Marketing

Meetup, Eventbrite, Constant Contact, FullCalendar.com

Benefit of Events

Events create a great platform to boost your business. Some benefits of having an event include:

- Reinforcement and enhancement of brand awareness - Throwing an event will help you get your company in the eye of more people.

- Lead generation - You are able to target people and follow up with them after the event.

- Creation of better relationships - Meet people who are interested in similar things as you and your business.

- Collaboration with others and development of partnerships - Increase what your event has to offer and offset some of the burden by getting other businesses involved.

- Letting your audience know what's going on - Use the Internet to publicize and make it easy for your audience to find out what's going on with your business. It can also be a reminder to people that you exist.

Key Learning - Focus on developing your pre-event strategies, day of event strategies and post event strategies. Each of these are critical components in creating a successful event.

Getting Started: Pre-Event Strategies

You have decided you want to do an event for your business, now what? I have hosted hundreds of events in the San Francisco Bay Area and beyond. Below I have created a list of actions for you to take in order to make your event a success.

1. **Securing a Space:** Choosing the right venue can be a difficult task. Before you start looking, lock in the number of guests that can attend your event. Keep in mind factors like whether it will be day or night, inside or outside, age range of guests, food and accommodations, etc. How far in advance is best to book your venue? Typically, 90 days or more is a good time to lock in a venue so you can start planning the rest of the event. Tip: start with a smaller venue and sell out.

2. **Creating a Strategy:** Before organizing and setting up the event, create a strategy that is clear and defined. Your strategy could include the following elements:

   • **Where**

      o Where will you hold the event? At the college campus, community center, local restaurant, country club?

      o Where will you promote the event (Online, Flyers, School Calendar, Community Groups, Alumni Newsletter)?

   • **When**

      o What time of the year will the event be held?

      o When will you time your announcements and invites?

- **What**
  - o What does success look like? How will you measure it?
  - o How many people do you expect?
  - o How long will the event be?
- **Who**
  - o How big will this event be?
  - o Who do you invite and how many people do you expect?
- **Budget**
  - o How much money will the event cost?
  - o What will be the cost for attending?
  - o What do you have available in your budget?
  - o How much will you need to spend on staffing resources?
- **Theme**
  - o What will the theme of your event be?
  - o Do you even need there be a theme?
  - o Do you need live music, what kind of ambiance do you want to create, will there be food/drink sampling, etc.?
- **Partnership & Sponsors**
  - o Will you partner with media, alumni, local associations, etc.?
  - o Will you collaborate with another company to help sponsor/run the event?

3. **Setting Up the Event:** The event web page is the central hub to the event. It is where the public can learn everything they need to know regarding the details of the event. Need help planning and promoting an upcoming event? There are two ways to set up an event online:

- **Create the Event Page Using Your Website:** The first option is to use your current website to create a webpage listing your event. Using your current website, you can create an "upcoming events" section to list your events on. If you do not have a website you want to use to host the event page, you can always create a new one using Wix or WordPress.

- **Create the Event Using an Event Creation Website:** The second option is to use Eventbrite or another form of event creation (if you don't have a website, this is an easy way to set up your event page). Using an online service can help you to plan, organize and promote any size event. What your event page could include:

  o Description

  o Location and time

  o How to register

  o Integrate of social media

  o Make it easy to tell multiple events apart (if you have other events listed on your page)

  Tip #1: Do not post two of the same event at once.

  Tip #2: Once your event page is published, if any major changes are made, they need to be announced through email.

  These event pages can help you reach a large audience and make your job a little bit easier.

4. **Ticket Registration:** After you have completed your event page, the next step is to create a ticket registration. However you set up the ticket registration, be sure to collect the attendees' information. You can decide how much information you want to collect from your attendees. Ideally, you want to collect attendee data that includes name, address, phone number, email, company, etc.

   In compiling the registration form, try not to ask too many questions. If the registration form is too complicated or time consuming, people won't want to go through the process of completing the registration. If you decide to charge a fee for attending the event, try to collect it on the spot. This makes for a seamless registration process and minimizes the check-in process on the day of the event by cutting down on collecting money at the door. Make sure a confirmation email goes out to the registrant as soon as possible. This ensures that the registration process is completed and that they have a receipt of the transaction.

If you are interested in collecting information on what is expected of the event, give registrants the option of completing a pre-event survey, asking what they want and expect from the event. This will help ensure you're providing value to your attendees.

5. **Securing Event Sponsors:** There are many different types of sponsors that can help by supporting your event. Some examples of sponsors include people or companies that donate paintings, trips, experiences, art for a silent auction, media sponsors that help promote an event, food sponsors that provide products/ services or assistance at the event, venue sponsors, local business sponsors, government sponsors and more.

Now that you have secured a space, created a strategy, set up your event webpage and have all of your materials in order, you can use all of that to put together an event sponsorship proposal. The proposal will outline a deal between you and the sponsor. Typically, in exchange for food, supplies, etc. for the event, you can offer free promotion of their products/services, tickets to the event or a table at the event.

6. **Promotion:** Once you've planned the event, the next step is to use a promotional mix of tools including the event page, email, social media, online event calendars and media sponsors to successfully get the word out about your event.

- Promote what you've got - An event can attract more business.

- Collaborate with others - Get other businesses and charities involved.

- Feature your calendar online - The Internet is a great way to publicize.

- Drive pre-event and post-event traffic to your social media and websites – This will create more brand awareness and interaction.

  Get the word out about your event by using sites that both empower event organizers to become more efficient and effective when bringing people together and allow you promote and track your attendance to see how many people are coming to your event. Improve the turnout of your event by communicating with your audience ahead of time. Your audience can be reached in several different ways including email, event calendars, partner promotions using media sponsors and social media.

- **Using Email to Promote an Event:** Email is a good place to start for the initial promotion of the event. Give your audience time to plan for the event by initiating contact around a month in advance.

- **Get Listed On Event Calendars:** Listing your event on sites like Fullcalendar.com will boost your event's web presence. Tools like FullCalendar are great for promoting an event, depending on your market.

- **Using Media Sponsors:** Another great way to promote your event is to get your media sponsors involved. Working with them to promote your event is a great way to reach a larger audience and increase the turnout. Your media sponsors can send emails to their audience and promote the event though their social media channels. Before your media sponsor promotes your event, provide them with a few guidelines to synchronize your marketing efforts with theirs in order to create a clear message.

- **Social Media for Event Promotion:** Events are current and by listing them online you can increase your visibility by showing up today in search engine and social media results. There are endless ways to use social media to promote your events and keep in touch with the attendees. To begin, you will need to create a marketing plan. The use of a marketing plan is to eliminate any confusion and to make sure that you always stay on the right track to reach the goal of your events.

o **Providing Updated Information About the Event:** Keep people updated with the latest news regarding your event, last minute changes, or general information that includes addresses, time/date, parking information and other helpful tips related to the event.

o **Engage the Attendees of the Event:** This can be done through creating countdowns to the event, promotions, quick links to the official website, allowing attendees to share photos, posting statuses with special hashtag (#) and other elements. You can also create competitions/raffles with prizes or other types of compensation.

o **Make use of YouTube videos:** Create an enticing video that people will share. You can post the teaser of your next event, any videos from past events, or even testimonials from people to capture the interest of those you wish to attend. Do not forget to make sure that the video is high-quality with excellent images, a clear voice and a catchy introduction.

o **Share, Share and Share:** Create custom social share buttons on your site to allow as many people as possible to share the event. Social share buttons consist of several sharing alternatives, including Like and Share on Facebook, LinkedIn, Google+ and other social media, as well as Tweeting on Twitter. These methods have been proven as a great way to drive traffic back to your promotional page.

o **Utilize Hashtags (#):** Hashtags are an effective and fun way to promote events. Come up with unique, catchy hashtags for attendees to use before or during each event.

They can be used on Twitter, Instagram and Facebook to raise awareness.

o **Follow Back/Socialize for Feedback:** Promoting doe not stop after the event has ended. Through social media you can follow up with the attendees, get feedback from them about what they liked best and least about the event and discover what people hope to see next time. In addition, you can use social media for pre-promotion for the next event.

Do not miss out on all the added value that can be created by utilizing the wonderful world of social media. We encourage you to be social and use all the capabilities of technology to promote your brand as well as events.

"Day of" Experience

Now that you have put in all the work for the pre-event strategies, the day of the event has finally come. On this day, print out a list of your attendees for the check-in process as the event starts. Check people in and confirm their information (name, email address, phone number, etc.). Collecting information from the event attendees is crucial for success. You want to be able to contact each and every person that attended. Be prepared to collect walk-in's information for those that show up and have not registered. Many attendees will bring their business cards to hand out at the event. You can collect these business cards for raffle or drawing.

Expect that not all of those who registered will actually show for the event. For a free event, you can expect that 40%-60% of RSVPs will show up. For a paid event, 85% of RSVPs will show up.

Key Tools: Although the preparation for the event is complete, the day of an event can be pretty hectic. Here are a few tips that can help to reduce any event malfunctions and further promote the event:

• **Volunteers:** It may be beneficial to have a few volunteers to help with setting up the event, greeting people and assisting you in making sure the event runs smoothly.

- **Thank your sponsors and attendees:** Remember to take the time out to thank the sponsors for supporting the event. You also want to thank the attendees for showing up. One way you can do this is by providing them with a complimentary discount or gift bag as a token of your appreciation. Check with your sponsors to see if they have something that can be donated for the gift bags to add value for the attendees.

- **Encourage use of social media:** Encourage event attendees to tweet, post on Instagram, check-in on Facebook and share their experience online. Create a unique, catchy hashtag for social media users to incorporate into their postings.

Post-Event Follow-Up Procedures

The event is over, but your job is not. If you want to maximize the effort you put into the event, following up is a key aspect.

1-2 Days Following the Event

- Send out a follow up email to all *REGISTERED* attendees, not just people who actually attended to thank them for attending. "We had a great turnout and a great event, thanks to our sponsors/volunteers etc." Be sure to address the guest by first name in the email (do this easily by using a platform such as Constant Contact or Mailchimp).

- If pictures were taken at the event, include at least one photo from the event in the email or let people know the pictures are coming soon.

- Provide an incentive to participate in a survey (ask what they liked about the event or what they would change about it). 'Thank you in advance for taking time to share your event experience with us'.

- Ask people to post, tweet and comment about their experience.

- Provide them with sample content. If you gave a presentation, offer to email a copy of the presentation.

- Network and regroup on your page. This will allow for greater interaction and communication.

- Emphasize a call to action. Why did you have the event? What did you want to get out of having the event?

- If you have another event coming up, feel free to mention it.

Event Promotion Checklist

- ❑ Does the business website feature a calendar of events?
- ❑ Is the Event calendar interactive?
- ❑ Is the calendar updated often?
- ❑ Does the business have a Meetup group? Sponsor a Meetup Group?
- ❑ Do events show up in Google searches?
- ❑ Does the business have an Eventbrite account?
- ❑ Does the business post events on Facebook?
- ❑ Does the business post events on Twitter?
- ❑ Are the events posted on local event sites? Eventbrite? FullCalendar?
- ❑ Is the business hosting "Fake" Q&A Events optimized for keywords?
- ❑ Does the business use event photos on their website?
- ❑ Does the business have a slideshow or video from event on website or video channel?

What's Your Score?

Rate your business based upon the answers to the previous questions.

How Many You Have		Score
0	=	0
1-3	=	30
4-6	=	60
7-9	=	80
10+	=	90

Your Event Marketing Score = _____

Suggestions, Tips & Tools

Events are a fun option to create more awareness surrounding your company, while simultaneously allowing you to build relationships with likeminded individuals. The following are sites that are helpful to plan and promote events.

Meetup for Business

Meetup.com is a useful site for people to promote their local business. The goal is to "revitalize local community and help people around the world self-organize." Meetup helps people to meet offline and save time and costs by inviting others to attend events. To date, Meetup has over 23 million members and is the world's largest network for local groups. It has around 9 million visitors every month, in 45,000 cities across 179 countries and 532,953 monthly meetups on every topic.[13] People use Meetup to find individuals with the same interests, to attend events and to promote their business. This is an easy and effective way for individuals to connect and network with

---

13 *See the Reference section at the end of the book for further information and sources*

one another. How do you successfully promote events on Meetup? Here are five helpful tips to get you started:

Create a Meetup Account: Pick a topic related to your business or an interest your target audience has. Create a detailed description of what you do, the kinds of members who would be interested and who would be a good fit to join your group. When creating a group, choose a narrow topic that is something unique to distinguish yourself from other similar groups in your area.

Organize regular meetups: As soon as you have created a group on Meetup, start organizing regular meetups such as workshops, seminars, or networking events sponsored by your business. Make sure your Meetup group has a number of members before organizing your first meetup.

Connect your Facebook to Meetup: Connecting your Facebook to Meetup is an easier way to promote what you have been organizing on your Meetup group. Your friends on Facebook will see what you are up to and vice versa.

Message your members: Once you gain a number of members, start messaging them about the upcoming events you are planning. Getting in touch with your members is a great way to keep them interested and active in your group.

Don't make it all about you and your business: Your guests are not planning on attending your event to hear all about what you do or what your business offers (even if you're the one who organized the meetup). They are interested in meeting individuals who share the same interest and bond over current issues of common interest. Give them a chance to speak and share thoughts, this will show that you genuinely care about them.

Being an organizer gives you the power of authority and allows you to demonstrate your capabilities as a business person. The purpose of organizing events is for your members to get to know you in person. People are more likely to do business with a person they like and respect. I organize networking meetups and have over 25 different targeted meetup groups. If you want to learn more about how to effectively promote events and maximize the use of Meetup, check

out my events website Professional Connector (www.professionalcon-
nector.com). You can come to one of my events to meet me and other
individuals who share the same interests that you do.

Eventbrite for Business

With Eventbrite's professional and customizable tools, planning
an event is made easy. Not only can you custom create your event, but
you can also access your event webpage anywhere using their easy to
use mobile application. Their services also give you the option to cross-
promote your event to any of your social media accounts. When using
Eventbrite, you can create a customized event registration page. After
you have completed your event page, the next step is to use Eventbrite
to create a ticket registration. Eventbrite will let you customize your
event's registration form so you can decide how much information
you want to collect from your attendees.

Need help spreading the word about your event? Eventbrite
makes getting the word out easy with personalized emails or adding
the events to search engines. Once your event is registered using
Eventbrite, you are given the option to send out emails to registered
attendees. After you have started promoting the event you can also
track your attendance to see how many people are coming to your
event, the ticket and registration sales and ramp up your professional
activity as needed.

Not only does Eventbrite help you plan and promote your event,
but it also helps manage event entry with their Entry Manager app
to check people in and scan barcoded tickets through your phone.
If that isn't for you, you can print out a guest list to check people in.
Eventbrite reaches a huge audience, makes life easier and helps to gain
traffic to your website.

Eventbrite is an all in one tool with everything you need to sell
tickets and manage registration of any kind of event. This is a great
option because it is a free and easy online tool that helps you create,
find and attend events. By using this online service, you can construct
any size event. With Eventbrite anyone can be a great event organizer.

It empowers event organizers to become more efficient and effective when bringing people together. People everywhere are searching Eventbrite to discover great events that matter to them.

RESOURCES
TECHNOLOGY TOOLS

Below is a partial list of products and solutions we have used with our consulting clients to streamline our client's business processes:

Constant Contact

Provides email, survey, etc system a variety of educational and motivational programs centered on business marketing, stock market investing, and real estate finance. Tactical Execution presents tactical to-do items people can use immediately to see immediate results. (https://piedmontconsulting.constantcontact.com)

vCita

Appointment Scheduler, Invoicing (www.bitly.com/vcita-piedmontave). Capture more clients and provide better service to your existing clients. vCita provides lead generation, online scheduling, and invoicing for small businesses all in one easy to use resource.

WP Engine

Hosted service provider, specifically tailored to WordPress websites and apps. (bit.ly/PACwpengine)

FreshBooks

Cloud-based accounting software service designed for owners of the types of small client-service businesses that send invoices to clients and get paid for their time and expertise. (http://shrsl.com/?~cdtd)

ZipRecruiter

A online job distribution and job board service. The web-based platform aggregates applications from job boards and provides tools for applicants tacking and screening. (bit.ly/pac-ziprecruiter)

SuperTasker

Outsource and manage high volumes of small tasks, super fast, to a pool of curated experts. SuperTasker uses intelligent algorithms to route the work to the most suited available taskers with a proven track record, so the work starts immediately. Delivery is time-boxed so you only pay for results, and the price is set dynamically based on availability and demand in real time. (www.supertasker.com)

Basecamp

Web-based project management tool. Basecamp offers to-do lists, wiki-style web-based text documents, milestone management, file sharing, time tracking, and a messaging system. Basecamp Classic also offers integration with Basecamp's own Campfire product, and features APIs that are used by a host of web and mobile apps. (http://bit.ly/basecampprojects)

Eventbrite

Global event marketplace for live experiences that allows people to find and create events in 190 countries. The platform allows event organizers to plan, promote, and sell tickets to events. It also enables attendees to find and purchase tickets to these experiences. (http://www.eventbrite.com/r/walnutcreekevents)

Bitly

Link management platform. Bitly shortens 600 million links per month,[2] for use in social networking, SMS, and email. (bit.ly/R5aB9v)

Wix

Website building platform used by millions of users. (bit.ly/wix-piedmontave)

Weebly

Website building platform used by millions of users. (http://shrsl.com/udyr)

RESOURCES
SMALL BUSINESS ADMINISTRATION

Government and Community

Every community has different free or low cost resources to help businesses get started and grow. Below are several agencies that provide services throughout the United States.

Small Business Administration

The Small Business Administration is a United States government agency that provides support to entrepreneurs and small businesses and every region of the country has an office. They can provide help with securing business loans, creating business plans and introductions to other federal, state and local government resources

Small Business Development Centers

America's SBDC represents America's nationwide network of Small Business Development Centers (SBDCs) – the most comprehensive small business assistance network in the United States and its territories. Hosted by leading universities, colleges and state economic development agencies, and funded in part by the United States Congress through a partnership with the U.S. Small Business Administration, nearly 1,000 service centers are available to provide no-cost business consulting and low-cost training. Small business owners and aspiring entrepreneurs can go to their local SBDCs for FREE face-to-face business consulting and at-cost training, on topics including writing business plans, accessing capital, marketing, regulatory compliance, technology development, international trade and more.

SCORE

For over 50 years, SCORE has served as America's premier source of free, confidential business education and mentoring. SCORE has over 300 chapters across the nation to help you succeed. Most mentors are experienced business owners and managers. They understand your challenges because they've faced them too. Your SCORE mentor can be both your coach and cheerleader to help you start or grow your business.

USING AS TEXTBOOK FOR TEACHING MARKETING AND BUSINESS COURSES

For the University of California, Berkeley and other colleges I have taught many courses, workshops and been a guest lecturer. The concepts and strategies outlined in this book have been used for one-day classes as well as for complete courses including a 30-hour, 10-week Marketing Strategy Course and a 15-hour, 5-week Marketing Strategy Course for the International Diploma Program at the University of California Extension. The strategies and tactics in this book help my students enhance their knowledge of business development, online technology and marketing strategy both in terms of theory and practice. If you email us at Info@PiedmontAve.com we are happy to discuss with you classroom curriculum and other supporting materials to make your course even better.

REFERENCES

23 days a year spent on your phone. (2016). *Mobilestatistics.com.* Retrieved 24 October 2016, from http://www.mobilestatistics.com/ mobile-news/23-days-a-year-spent-on-your-phone.aspx

Ames, E. (2016). *Infographic: Survey Identifies Social Selling as Key Revenue Generator. Ama.org.* Retrieved 24 October 2016, from https://www.ama.org/publications/MarketingNews/Pages/social-selling-2016-infographic-sales-for-life.aspx

Bennett, S. (2012). *How Much Time And Money Do Small Businesses Spend On Social Media? [INFOGRAPHIC]. Adweek.com.* Retrieved 24 October 2016, from http://www.adweek.com/socialtimes/ smb-social-media/472057

Twitter (2016). *About.twitter.com.* Retrieved 24 October 2016, from https://about.twitter.com/company

Ewer, T. (2014). *14 Surprising Statistics About WordPress Usage - ManageWP. ManageWP.* Retrieved 24 October 2016, from https:// managewp.com/14-surprising-statistics-about-wordpress-usage

Yelp. (2016). *Yelp.* Retrieved 24 October 2016, from https:// www.yelp.com/factsheet

Grimes, M. (2012). *Nielsen: Global Consumers' Trust in 'Earned' Advertising Grows in Importance | Nielsen. Nielsen.com.* Retrieved

24 October 2016, from http://www.nielsen.com/us/en/
press-room/2012/nielsen-global-consumers-trust-in-earned-advertis-
ing-grows.html

Hitz, L. (2014). *Influencer Marketing: Stats and Quotes
You Need to Know. Simply Measured.* Retrieved 24
October 2016, from http://simplymeasured.com/blog/
influencer-marketing/#sm.000014585ugufcco7wioxrbp9ga2r

Instagram: active users (2016) | Statista. (2016). *Statista.* Retrieved
24 October 2016, from https://www.statista.com/statistics/253577/
number-of-monthly-active-instagram-users/

Kessler, G. (2014). *Do nine out of 10 new businesses fail, as Rand Paul
claims?. Washington Post.* Retrieved 24 October 2016, from https://
www.washingtonpost.com/news/fact-checker/wp/2014/01/27/
do-9-out-of-10-new-businesses-fail-as-rand-paul-claims/

Kingwill, I. (2015). *What is the Cost of Customer
Acquisition vs Customer Retention?. LinkedIn.* Retrieved
24 October 2016, from https://www.linkedin.com/pulse/
what-cost-customer-acquisition-vs-retention-ian-kingwill

*Marketing Statistics, Trends & Data - The Ultimate List of Marketing
Stats.* (2016). *Hubspot.com.* Retrieved 24 October 2016, from http://
www.hubspot.com/marketing-statistics

Marrs, M. (2016). *What is Mobile Marketing and Why Does it
Matter? (So So Much!). Wordstream.com.* Retrieved 24 October
2016, from http://www.wordstream.com/blog/ws/2013/08/19/
what-is-mobile-marketing

Mitroff, I. I., Shrivastava, P., & Udwadia, F. E. (1987). *Effective
crisis management.* Emmitsburg, MD: National Emergency Training
Center.

Mitroff, S. R., Cain, M. S., & Clark, K. (2015). *Perception
and Human Information Processing in Visual Search.* Cambridge
University Press.

Mitroff, D. D., & Mitroff, I. I. (2012). *Fables and the Art of Leadership: Applying the Wisdom of Mister Rogers to the Workplace.* Palgrave Macmillan.

Pick, T. (2016). *47 Superb Social Media Marketing Stats and Facts. Business 2 Community.* Retrieved 24 October 2016, from http://www.business2community.com/social-media/47-superb-social-media-marketing-stats-facts-01431126#pov piIQERBhD4oHV.97

LinkedIn. (2016). *Linkedin.com.* Retrieved 24 October 2016, from https://www.linkedin.com/static?key=pop% 2Fpop_more_profile_completeness

Shah, P. (2015). *How To Use Meetup.com To Promote A Local Business. Business 2 Community.* Retrieved 24 October 2016, from http://www.business2community.com/social-media/ how-to-use-meetup-com-to-promote-a-local-business-01331445#GTh9RqQbOY7vhIXi.97

Silvers, D. M. (2017). Five mistakes of beginning design thinkers (and how to overcome them). Retrieved from https://www.linkedin. com/pulse/five-mistakes-beginning-design-thinkers-how-over-come-mitroff-silvers/.

Social Media: The Basics for B2b. (2011). *Nurture Marketing.* Retrieved 24 October 2016, from http://www.nurturemarketing. com/sites/default/files/SocialMedia.pdf

Statistics - YouTube. (2016). *Youtube.com.* Retrieved 24 October 2016, from https://www.youtube.com/yt/press/statistics.html

Statistics and facts about Social Media Marketing in the United States. (2016). *www.statista.com.* Retrieved 24 October 2016, from https:// www.statista.com/topics/1538/social-media-marketing/

Sterling, G. (2016). *Nearly 80 percent of social media time now spent on mobile devices. Marketing Land.* Retrieved

24 October 2016, from http://marketingland.com/
facebook-usage-accounts-1-5-minutes-spent-mobile-171561

Stych, J. (2016). *What is Drip Marketing? The Complete
Guide to Drip Campaigns, Lifecycle Emails, and More - The
Ultimate Guide to Email Marketing Apps. Zapier.com.*
Retrieved 1 November 2016, from https://zapier.com/learn/
ultimate-guide-to-email-marketing-apps/drip-marketing-campaign/

Top 20 Facebook Statistics - Updated July 2016. (2016). *Zephoria
Inc..* Retrieved 24 October 2016, from https://zephoria.com/
top-15-valuable-facebook-statistics/

Twitter: number of active users 2010-2016. (2016). *Statista.* Retrieved
24 October 2016, from https://www.statista.com/statistics/282087/
number-of-monthly-active-twitter-users/

73494621R00093

Made in the USA
San Bernardino, CA
07 April 2018